The Complete Distiller: Containing, I. the Method of Performing the Various Processes of Distillation, ... Iii. the Method of Making All the Compound Waters and Rich Cordials ... to Which Are Added, Accurate Descriptions of the Several Drugs, Plants, ...

Ambrose Cooper

THE

COMPLETE

DISTILLER.

L

Fig. 9.

c

Fig. 8.

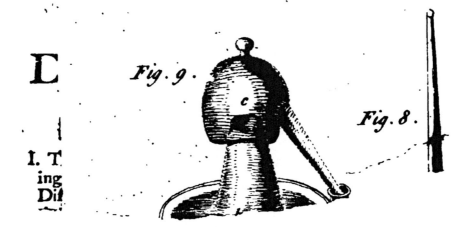

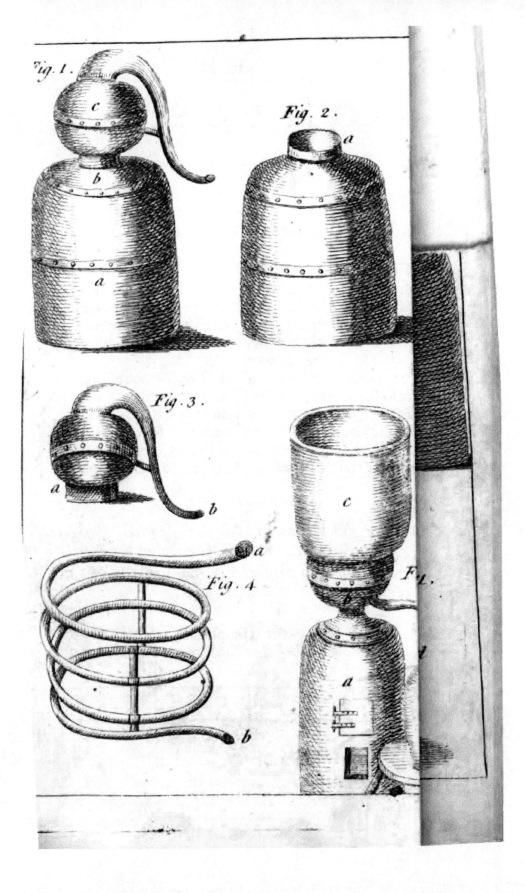

THE
COMPLETE
DISTILLER:

CONTAINING,

I. The Method of performing the various Proceſſes of Diſtillation, with Deſcriptions of the ſeveral Inſtruments: The whole Doctrine of Fermentation: The manner of drawing Spirits from Malt, Raiſins, Moloſſes, Sugar, &c. and of rectifying them: With Inſtructions for imitating to the greateſt Perfection both the Colour and Flavour of *French* Brandies.

II. The manner of diſtilling all Kinds of Simple Waters from Plants, Flowers, &c.

III. The Method of making all the compound Waters and rich Cordials ſo largely imported from *France* and *Italy*; as likewiſe all thoſe now made in *Great Britain*.

To which are added,

Accurate Deſcriptions of the ſeveral Drugs, Plants, Flowers, Fruits, &c. uſed by Diſtillers, and Inſtructions for chuſing the beſt of each Kind.

The Whole delivered in the plaineſt manner, for the Uſe both of *Diſtillers* and *Private Families*.

By *A. COOPER*, DISTILLER.

LONDON:

Printed for P. VAILLANT in the *Strand*; and R. GRIFFITHS in *Pater-Noſter-Row*.

M.DCC.LVII.

THE
PREFACE.

IT is now some Years since I first formed a Design of compiling a complete System of Distillation; and accordingly read most of the Treatises on that Subject, and extracted from each what I thought necessary for my Purpose, proposing to supply the Defects from my own Experience. It is, however, more than probable, that this Design had never been executed, had not a French Treatise of Distillation* fell

A 3

into

* This Treatise is intitled *Traité Raisonné de la Distillation*; *ou La Distillation réduite en Principes*: *Avec un Traité des Odeurs. Par M. DE'JEAN, Distillateur.* Printed at *Paris*, in the Year, M.DCC.LIII.

PREFACE.

into my Hands; but finding in that Book many useful Observations, and a great Number of Recipes for making various Sorts of compound Waters and Cordials, I determined to finish the Work I had begun, being now enabled to render it much more useful than it was possible for me otherwise to have done. What I have translated from this Author, will, I dare say, be kindly received by our Distillers, as the manner of making many of the foreign Compound Waters, &c. has never before been published in the English Language. And I flatter myself, if the several Hints interspersed through this Treatise are carefully adverted to, Distillation may be carried to a much greater Degree of Perfection than it is at present; and the celebrated Compound Waters and Cordials of the French and Italians, imported at so great an Expence, and such Detriment to the Trade of this Nation,

PREFACE.

Nation, may be made in England, equal to those manufactured abroad.

My principal Intention being to render this Treatise useful to all, I have endeavoured to deliver every thing in the plainest and most intelligible Manner. Beauty of Stile is not, indeed, to be expected in a Work of this Nature; and therefore if Perspicuity be not wanting, I presume the Reader will forgive me, if he meets with some Passages that might have been delivered in a more elegant Manner. I have also, for the same Reason, avoided, as much as possible, Terms of Art, and given all the Recipes in Words at length.

Distillation, tho' long practised, has not been carried to the Degree of Perfection that might reasonably have been expected. Nor will this

A 4

PREFACE.

this appear surprizing, if it be confidered, that the Generality of Diſtillers proceed in the ſame beaten Track, without hardly ſuſpecting their Art capable of Improvements; or giving themſelves any Trouble to enquire into the Rationale of the ſeveral Proceſſes they daily perform. They imagine, that the Theory of Diſtillation is very abſtruſe, and above the Reach of common Capacities; or, at leaſt, that it requires a long and very aſſiduous Study to comprehend it; and, therefore, content themſelves with repeating the Proceſſes, without the leaſt Variation. This Opinion, however ridiculous it may appear to thoſe not acquainted with the preſent Practice of Diſtillers, has, I am ſatisfied, been the principal Cauſe why Diſtillation has not been carried to the Height it would otherwiſe have been. I have therefore endeavoured in the following Treatiſe to deſtroy this idle Opinion, and ſhew

the

PREFACE.

the Distiller how he may proceed on rational Principles, and direct his Enquiries in such a manner as cannot fail of leading him to such Discoveries in his Profession, as will be attended with Advantage both to himself and his Country.

But it is not to those only who make Distillation their Profession, that I have laboured to render this Treatise useful; I have also endeavoured to extend its Utility to those who distil Simple and Compound Waters for their own Use, or to distribute to their indigent Neighbours. And for this Reason I have adapted most of the Recipes to small Quantities, and briefly enumerated the Virtues and Uses of each Composition.

The short Descriptions of the most capital Ingredients, and the Directions for chusing the best of each Kind,

PREFACE.

Kind, I flatter myself will not be considered as improper: Because the Goodness of every Composition, must, in a great Measure, depend on the Goodness of the Ingredients.

As Typographical Errors are almost impossible to be avoided, the Reader will, I hope, pardon any he may chance to meet with in the ensuing Treatise; and the rather as, I dare say, there are none but what he may himself very easily correct.

THE

THE
CONTENTS.

PART I.

Of the Diſtillation of Spirits.

X.

CONTENTS.

PART

CONTENTS,

PART. II.

Containing the Method of distilling Simple Waters.

CONTENTS.

PART III.

Of making Compound Waters and Cordials.

CONTENTS.

CONTENTS.

THE

A

Complete System

OF

DISTILLATION.

DISTILLATION is the Art of feparating, or drawing off the fpirituous,
aqueous, and oleaginous Parts of a
mixt Body from the groffer, and more ter-
reftrial Parts, by means of Fire, and con-
denfing them again by Cold.

We fhall therefore divide this Treatife
into three Parts; in the firft, we fhall explain the Method of diftilling Spirits from
various Subftances; in the fecond, the manner of drawing fimple Waters; and in the
third, the beft Methods of making cordial
or compound Waters.

PART I.

Of the Diſtillation of Spirits.

BY the Diſtillation of Spirits is to be underſtood the Art by which all inflammable Spirits, Brandies, Rums, Arracks, and
the like, are procured from vegetable Subſtances, by the means of a previous Fermentation, and a ſubſequent Treatment of
the fermented Liquor by the Alembic, or
hot Still, with its proper Worm and Refrigeratory.

But as it is impoſſible to extract vinous
Spirits from any vegetable Subject without
Fermentation, and previous to this Brewing
is often neceſſary, it will be requiſite firſt to
conſider theſe Operations.

CHAP. I.

Of Brewing, in order to the Production of inflammable Spirits.

BY Brewing, we mean the extracting a
Tincture from ſome vegetable Subſtance, or diſſolving it in hot Water, by
which means it becomes proper for a vinous
Fermentation.

A

A Solution, or fermentable Tincture of this kind, may be procured, with proper Management, from any vegetable Subſtance, but the more readily and totally it diſſolves in the Fluid, the better it is fitted for Fermentation, and the larger its Produce of Spirits. All inſpiſſated vegetable Juices therefore, as Sugar, Honey, Treacle, Manna, &c. are very proper for this Uſe, as they totally diſſolve in Water, forming a clear and uniform Solution ; but Malt, for its Cheapneſs, is generally preferred in *England*, though it but imperfectly diſſolves in hot Water. The worſt ſort is commonly choſen for this Purpoſe ; and the Tincture, without the Addition of Hops, or Trouble of boiling it, is directly cooled and fermented.

But in order to brew with Malt to the greateſt Advantage, the three following Particulars ſhould be carefully attended to : 1. the Subject ſhould be well prepared ; that is, it ſhould be juſtly malted, and well ground : For if it be too little malted, it will prove hard and flinty ; and conſequently, only a ſmall Part of it diſſolve in the Water : And, on the other hand, if too much malted, a great Part of the finer Particles, or fermentable Matter, will be loſt in the Operation. With regard to grinding, the Malt

B 2 ſhould

should be reduced to a kind of coarse Meal; for Experience has shewn, that by this means, the whole Substance of the Malt may, through the whole Process, continue mixed with the Tincture, and be distilled with it; whereby a larger Quantity of Spirit will be obtained, and also great Part of the Trouble, Time and Expence in Brewing saved. This Secret depends upon thoroughly mixing, or briskly agitating the Meal, first in cold Water, and then in hot; and repeating this Agitation after the Fermentation is finished: When the thick turbid Wash must be immediately committed to the Still. And thus the two Operations of Brewing and Fermenting may very commodiously be reduced to one, to the no small Profit and Advantage of the Distiller.

The second Particular to be attended to, is, that the Water be good, and properly applied. Rain Water is the best adapted to Brewing; for it not only extracts the Tincture of the Malt better than any other; but also abounds in fermentable Parts, whereby the Operation is quickened, and the Yield of the Spirit increased. The next to that of Rain, is the Water of Rivers and Lakes, particularly such as wash any large Tract of a fertile Country, or receive the Sullage of populous Towns. But

whatever

whatever Water is uſed, it muſt ſtand in a hot State upon the prepared Malt, eſpecially if a clear Tincture be deſired; but the greateſt Care muſt be taken to prevent the Malt from running into Lumps or Clods; and, indeed, the beſt Way to prevent this, is to put a ſmall Quantity of cold Water to the Malt firſt, and mix them well together; after which the remaining Quantity of Water may be added in a State of boiling, without the leaſt Danger of coagulating the Malt, or what the Diſtillers call, making a Pudding.

It has been found by Experience, that a certain Degree of Heat is neceſſary to extract the whole Virtue of the Malt: This Degree may, by the above Method, be determined to the greateſt Exactneſs, as the Heat of boiling Water may at once be leſſened to any aſſigned Degree of Warmth, by a proper Addition of cold Water; due Regard being had to the Seaſon of the Year, and the Temperature of the Air. This Improvement, with that mentioned above, of reducing the two Operations of Brewing and Fermentation to one, will be attended with conſiderable Advantage.

With regard to the proper Quantity of Water, it muſt be obſerved, that it too little be uſed, a viſcid clammy Mixture will be

B 3 produced,

produced, little difpofed to ferment, nor capable of extracting all the foluble Parts of the Malt. On the other hand, too much Water renders the Tincture thin and aqueous, and by that means increafes the Trouble and Expence in all Parts of the Operation. A due Medium, therefore, fhould be chofen; and Experience has fhewn, that a Wafh about the Goodnefs of that defigned by the *London* Brewers for Ten Shilling Beer, will beft anfwer the Diftiller's Purpofe. When a proper Quantity of Water is mixed with the Malt, the whole Mafs muft be well agitated, that all the foluble Parts of the Malt may often come in contact with the aqueous Fluid, which being well faturated after ftanding a proper time, muft be drawn off, frefh Water poured on, and the Agitations repeated, till at laft the whole Virtue, or faccharine Sweetnefs of the Malt is extracted, and only a fixed hufky Matter remains, incapable of being diffolved by either hot or cold Water.

The third requifite Particular is, that fome certain Additions be ufed, or Alterations made according to the Seafon of the Year, or the Intention of the Operator. The Seafon of the Year is very neceffary to be confidered. In the Summer, the Water applied to the Malt muft be colder than in the Winter; and in hot fultry Weather,

the

the Tincture muſt be ſuddenly cooled, otherwiſe it will turn eager ; and, in order to
check the too great Tendency it has to Fermentation, when the Air is hot, it will be
neceſſary to add a proper Quantity of un-
malted Meal, which being much leſs diſpoſed to Fermentation than Malt, will
greatly moderate its Impetuoſity, and render
the Operation ſuitable to the Production of
Spirits, which, by a too violent Fermentation, would, in a great Meaſure, be diſſi-
pated and loſt.

C H A P. II.

Of Fermentation.

THE Tincture, or, as the Diſtillers call
it, the Waſh, being prepared, as in
the foregoing Chapter, it is next to be fermented ; for, without this Operation, no
vinous Spirit can be produced.

By Fermentation is meant that inteſtine
Motion performed by the inſtrumental Efficacy of Water, whereby the Salt, Oil and
Earth of a fermentable Subject, are ſepa-
rated, attenuated, tranſpoſed, and again
collected, and recompoſed in a particular
Manner.

The Doctrine of Fermentation, is of the greatest Use, and should be well understood by every Distiller, as it is the very Basis of the Art; and, perhaps, if more attended to, a much purer Spirit, as well as a greater Quantity of it, might be procured from the same Materials than at present. We shall therefore lay down a concise Theory of Fermentation, before we proceed to deliver the Practice.

Every fermentable Subject is composed of Salt, Oil, and a subtile Earth; but these Particles are so small, that, when asunder, they are imperceptable to the Senses; and, therefore, when mixed with an aqueous Fluid, they leave it transparent; neither have fermentable Bodies any Taste, except that of Sweetness.

These Particles are each composed of Salt, Oil and Earth, intimately mixed in an actual Cohesion, Connexion, and Union; and, therefore, when any one of those Principles, too much abounds in any Subject, so that an intimate Union is prevented, the whole Efficacy of the Fermentation is either stopped or impaired, or at least limited to one certain Species.

This

This equal Connexion of Salt, Oil and Earth into a ſingle compound Particle, forms a Corpuſcle ſoluble in Water ; or, to ſpeak more philoſophically, this compound Corpuſcle is, by means of its ſaline Particles, connected with the aqueous Corpuſcles, and moved up and down with them. But where theſe Corpuſcles are not thus connected with the Water, a Number of them join together, and form either a groſs, or a looſe, chaffy, and ſpungy Matter.

When theſe compound Particles are diluted with a ſmall Quantity of an aqueous Fluid, they feel ſlippery, clammy, and unctuous to the Touch, and affect the Taſte with a kind of ropy Sweetneſs. And when a proper Quantity of the Fluid is added, a Commotion is preſently excited, and afterwards a ſubtile Separation.

This Commotion and Separation firſt begins in the whole Subſtance ; for before the Addition of Water, the Subject may remain in dry, ſolid, and large Pieces, as in Malt, Sugar, &c. which being reduced to Powder, each Grain thereof is an Aggregate of many ſmaller compound Corpuſcles ; theſe being put into Water, diſſolve, and ſeparately float therein, till at length, they become

come fo fmall as to be invifible, and only thicken the Confiftence of the Liquor.

These Corpufcles being thus feparated from one another, there next enfues a Separation of their component Particles ; that is, the Salt, the Oil, and the Earth, are divided by the Interpofition of the aqueous Particles.

The firft Commotion is no more than a bare Solution ; for the faline Particles being eafily diffolvable in Water, they are immediately laid hold of by the aqueous Particles, and carried about with them. But the fucceeding Separation, or fermentative Motion, is a very different thing ; for by this the faline Particles are divided from thofe of Oil and Earth, partly by the Impulfe of the others in their Motion, and partly by the Force of the aqueous Particles, which are now continually meeting and dafhing againft them.

This Motion is performed by the Water, as a Fluid, or Aggragate of an infinite Number of Particles, in actual and perpetual Motion ; their Smallnefs being proportionable to that of the fermenting Corpufcles, and their Motion, or conftant Sufceptibility of Motion, by Warmth, and the Motion of the Air, difpofing them to move

other

other ſubtile moveable Corpuſcles alſo. The certain Agreement of Figure, or Size between the aqueous Particles, and thoſe of the Salt in the fermentable Subject, tends greatly to increaſe this Commotion ; for, by this means, they are readily and very cloſely connected together ; and therefore move almoſt like one and the ſame compound Corpuſcle ; whilſt the Water is not at all diſpoſed to cohere immediately with either the Oil or Earth. And thus an unequal Concuſſion is excited in the compound Corpuſcles of the fermentable Subject ; which Concuſſion at length ſtrikes out the ſaline Particle, looſens the others, and finally produces a Separation of the original Connexion of the Subject.

An aqueous Fluid, therefore, is the true, and indeed the only, Inſtrument for procuring a fermentable Motion in theſe compound Corpuſcles of the Subject : For were an oily Fluid poured upon any fermentable Subject, no vinous Fermentation would enſue ; as the Oil could neither give a ſufficient Impulſe on the compound Corpuſcles, which are groſſer than its own conſtituent Particles, nor divide the oily or ſaline Particles of the Subject from their Connexion with the others, which detain, and, as it were, envelope, or defend them from its Action.

The

The compound Corpuscles of the fermentable Subject being affected by the perpetual Motion of the Particles of the aqueous Fluid, a proper Degree of Motion is necessary, or that the Particles move with a proper Degree of Velocity, which principally depends on external Heat. A considerable Degree of Cold, indeed, will not absolutely prevent Fermentation, though it will greatly retard it; and a boiling Heat will prevent it still more. A tepid, or middle Degree of Heat between Freezing or Boiling, is therefore the most proper for promoting and quickening the Operation.

The Admission of Air, also, though not of absolute Necessity, yet greatly promotes and quickens the Action, as being a capital Instrument in putting in a proper Degree of Motion the oily Particles of the Subject. But whilst the Air thus contributes to hasten the Effect, it causes at the same time by its Activity some remarkable Alterations in the oily Particles; for it not only moves, but absolutely dissolves and displaces them from their original Connexions; and thus carries them off with itself from the whole Mass. And, therefore, though the Consideration of the Air does not so properly belong to Fermentation in the general, yet it does in particular; as having an accidental Power to to alter every Species of this Operation ; Confequently its Agency ought to be well underftood, either to procure Alterations at pleafure in the fermenting Mafs, or to prevent and correct impending Dangers.

The oily Particles thus feparated and diffolved by the Air, are alfo elaftic, though they probably derive that Property from their Intercourfe with the Air itfelf, and their being rendered extremely minute.

When, therefore, an aqueous Fluid is added to a fermentable Subject expofed to a temperate Heat, a fermentative Struggle immediately arifes, the faline Part of the compound Particles being diffolved by the continual inteftine Motion of the Water, and carried up and down with it in all Directions, amidft an infinite Number of other Particles, as well fermentable, as aqueous ones ; whence, by this Collifion and Attrition, the faline Particles are diffolved, and feparated from their Connexion with the oily and earthy. And as the oily Particles are the moft fubtle and elaftic, they would, by this means, be thrown up to the Surface of the Liquor, and carried off by the Air, were they not clofely connected with the earthy ones, whofe Gravity prevents their Evaporation, and, by coming in contact with others of the fame kind, form

Aggregations,

Aggregations, and sink down, with the oily Particles, to the Bottom. But before these can form a Bulk too large to be supported by the Water, many of the oily Particles are, by their frequent Collisions with the aqueous Fluid, separated from the earthy ones; and, by Degrees, more strongly connected again with the saline ones; whilst, on the other hand, the same saline Particles imbibe some of the earthy ones, which being left single, upon their Separation from the oily Particles, floated about separately in the Fluid.

And hence proceed the several different Consequences of Fermentation; *viz.* 1. From the Separation of the saline Particles of the fermentable Subject proceeds the tart, saline, or acid Taste of the Liquor; which is more sensible at first, before the Liquor is duly composed and settled, or the due Arrangement and Connection of the saline Particles with those of the oily and earthy Kinds, completed : After which the Liquor proves milder, softer, or less pungent. 2. From the oily Particles being set at liberty, proceeds the strong Smell of the Liquor, and the Head or shining Skin upon the Surface. 3. The earthy Particles collecting together in Clusters, cause the Fluid to appear turbid, and afterwards a visible earthy, or clay-like Matter to be precipitated : And

some

fome of the earthy Parts, in their Motion, arriving at the Head, or oily Skin on the Surface, caufe it to thicken; and afterwards taking it down along with it, thus confti- tute the Lees which abound in Oil. 4. From this new Struggle or Colliſion, which is pro- ductive both of Solution, and a new Con- nection in the faline and earthy Corpufcles, proceeds the Ebullition in Fermentation. And, laftly, by the fame repeated Coalition of the oily with the aqueous and faline Particles, the inflammable Spirit is pro- duced.

Having thus laid down a concife Theory of Fermentation, we fhall now proceed to the Practice.

The Wafh being brought to a tepid, or luke- warm State in the Backs, a proper Quantity of a good-conditioned Ferment is added; but if the Ferment be folid, it fhould be previ- oufly broke into fmall Pieces, and gently thinned either with the Hand, Whifp, &c. in a little of the tepid Liquor. A complete and uniform Solution, however, fhould not be attempted, becaufe that would greatly weaken the Power of the Ferment, or de- ftroy its future Efficacy. The whole in- tended Quantity, therefore, being thus loofely mixed with a moderate Parcel of the Liquor, and kept in a tepid State, either

by

by setting it near the Fire, or otherwise, and free from the too rude Commerce of the external Air; more of the insensibly warm Liquor ought to be added, at proper Intervals, till, at length, the whole Quantity is properly set to working together. And, thus, by dividing the Business into Parts, it may much more speedily and effectually be performed, than by attempting it all at once.

The whole Quantity of Liquor being thus set to work, secured in a proper Degree of Warmth, and defended from a too free Intercourse of the external Air, Nature itself, as it were, finishes the Process, and renders the Liquor fit for the Still.

By Ferments, we mean any Substance, which, being added to any rightly disposed fermentable Liquor, will cause it to ferment much sooner and faster than it would of itself; and, consequently, render the Operation shorter; in contradiction to those abusively called so, which only correct some Fault in the Liquor, or give it some Flavour. Hence we see, that the principal Use of Ferments is to save Time, and make Dispatch in Business; whilst they only occasionally, and, as it were, by Accident, give a Flavour, and increase the Quantity of Spirit. And, accordingly, any fermentable
Liquor,

Liquor, may, without the Addition of any Ferment, by a proper Management of Heat alone, be brought to ferment, and even more perfectly, though much flower, than with their Affiftance.

These Ferments are, in general, the Flowers and Fæces of all fermentable Liquors, generated and thrown to the Surface, or depofited at the Bottom, either during the Act of Fermentation, or after the Operation is finifhed.

Two of thefe are procurable in large Quantities, and at a fmall Expence; we mean, Beer-Yeaft and Wine-Lees; a prudent and artificial Management, or Ufe of which, might render the Bufinefs of Diftillation much more facile, certain and advantageous.

It has been efteemed very difficult, and a great Difcouragement, in the Bufinefs of Diftillation, to procure a fufficient Stock of thefe Materials, and preferve them at all times ready for ufe. The whole Secret confifts in dexteroufly freeing the Matter from its fuperfluous Moifture; becaufe in its fluid State, it is fubject to a farther Fermentation, which is productive of Corruption; in which State it becomes intollerably fœtid and cadaverous.

C   The

The Method of expofing it to the Air till it has required a proper Confiftence, is fubject to great Inconveniencies; and fo peculiar and careful a Management neceffary, that it rarely fucceeds.

The beft Way, therefore, is to prefs it very flowly and gradually, in a thick, clofe, and ftrong Canvas Bag, after the manner of Wine Lees, by the Tail prefs, till it becomes a kind of Cake; which, though foft, will eafily fnap, or break dry and brittle between the Fingers. Being reduced to that Confiftence, and clofely packed up in a tight Cafk, it will remain a long Time uncorrupted, preferve its Fragrancy, and confequently, fit to be ufed for fermenting the fineft Liquor.

The fame Method is alfo practicable, and to the fame Advantage, in the Flowers or Yeaft of Wine; which may be thus commodioufly imported from abroad: Or, if thefe cannot be procured, others of equal Efficacy may be procured from frefh Wine Lees, by barely mixing and ftirring them into a proper warm Liquor; whence the lighter, or more volatile and active Parts of the Lees, will be thrown to the Surface, and may eafily be taken off, and preferved, by the above-mentioned Method, in any

desired

desired Quantity. And hence, by a very
easy Process, an inexhaustible Supply of the
most useful Ferments may be readily and
successively procured, so as to prevent for
the future all Occasion of Complaint for
want of them, in the Distiller's Business.

Experience has demonstrated, that all
Ferments abound much more in essential
Oil, than the Liquor which produced them;
and consequently they retain, in a very high
Degree, the Smell and Flavour of the Sub-
ject. It is therefore requisite, before the
Ferment is applied, to consider what Fla-
vour is intended to be introduced, or what
Species of Ferment is most proper for the
Liquor.

The Alteration thus caused by Ferments
is so considerable, as to render any neutral
fermentable Liquor, of the same Flavour
with that which yielded the Ferment. This
Observation is of much greater Moment
than will presently be conceived ; for a new
Scene is hereby opened, both in the Business of Distillation, and others depending
upon Fermentation. It must, however, be
observed, that its Benefit does not extend
to Malt, treated in the common Method ;
nor to any other Subject but what affords
a Spirit tolerably pure and tasteless : For,
otherwise, instead of producing a simple,

C 2 pure;

pure, and uniform Flavour, it causes a compound, mixed, and unnatural one. How far the fine Stiller may profit by it, well deserves his Attention ; and whether our native Cyder Spirit, Crab Spirit, &c. which have very little Flavour of their own, may not, by this Artifice, be brought nearly, if not intirely, into the State of some foreign Brandies, so highly esteemed, is recommended to Experience.

It is common with Distillers, in order to increase the Quantity of Spirit, give it a particular Flavour, or improve its Vinosity, to add several things to the Liquor, during the Time it is in a State of Fermentation; and these Additions may properly be reduced to Salts, Acids, Aromatics, and Oils.

All rich vegetable Juices, as Treacle, Honey, &c. which either want a natural Acid, have been deprived of it, or contain it in too small a Quantity, will be greatly improved by adding, at the Beginning of the Operation, a small Quantity of the vegetable or fine mineral Acids ; as Oil of Sulphur, Glauber's Spirit of Salt, Juice of Lemons, or an aqueous Solution of Tartar. These Additions will either give, or greatly improve the vinous Acidity of the Subject, but not increase the Quantity of the Spirit,

that

that Intention being performed by Aromatics and Oils.

All pungent Aromatics have a furprifing Quality of increafing the Quantity of the Spirit, as well as in altering, or improving the Flavour; but their Ufe requires that the Fermentation fhould be performed in clofe Veffels. And if a large Quantity be intended to be added, Care muft be taken not to do it all at once, left the Oilinefs of the Ingredients fhould check the Operation. But if the Flavour be the principal Intention, they fhould not be added till the Operation is nearly finifhed. After the fame Manner a very confiderable Quantity of any effential vegetable Oil may be converted into a furprifingly large Quantity of inflammable Spirit; but great Caution is here alfo neceffary not to drop it too faft, or add too large a Quantity at a time, which would damp the Fermentation; it being the fureft Method of checking, or totally ftopping this Operation, at any Point of Time required. The beft Method, therefore, of adding the Oil, fo as to avoid all Inconveniencies, is to rub the Oil in a Mortar with Sugar, which the Chemifts call making an *Olæofaccharum*, by which Means the Tenacity of the Oil will be deftroyed, and the whole readily mix with the Liquor, and immediately ferment with it. The Diftiller would do well

to

to confider thefe Obfervations attentively, as he may thence form an advantageous Method of increafing the Quantity of Spirits, and at the fame Time greatly improve their Quality and Flavour.

But in order to put thefe Obfervations in practice, particular Regard muft be had to the containing Veffel in which the Fermentation is performed, the Exclufion of the Air, and the Degree of the external Heat or Cold.

With regard to the containing Veffel; its Purity, and the Provifion for rendering it occafionally clofe, are chiefly to be confidered. In cleanfing it, no Soap, or other unctuous Body fhould be ufed, for fear of checking the Fermentation; and, for the fame Reafon, all ftrong alkaline Lixiviums fhould be avoided. Lime-water, or a turbid Solution of quick Lime may be employed for this Purpofe, without producing any ill Effect; it will alfo be of great Service in deftroying a prevailing acetous Salt, which is apt to generate in the Veffels when the warm Air has free Accefs to them; and tends to pervert the Order of Fermentation, and, inftead of a Wine or Wafh, produce a Vinegar. Special Care muft alfo be had, that no Remains of Yeaft, or cadaverous Remains of former fermented Matters, hang

about

about the Veſſels, which would infect whatever ſhould be afterwards put into them; and cannot, without the utmoſt Difficulty, be perfectly cured and ſweetened.

The occaſional Cloſeneſs of the Veſſels may in the large way, be provided for by Covers properly adapted; and, in the ſmall way, by Valves, placed in light Caſks. Theſe Valves will occaſionally give the neceſſary Vent to preſerve the Veſſel, during the Height of the Fermentation; the Veſſel otherwiſe remaining perfectly cloſe, and impervious to the Air.

It is a Miſtake of a very prejudicial Nature, in the Buſineſs of Fermentation, to ſuppoſe, that there is an abſolute Neceſſity for a free Admiſſion of the external Air. The expreſs contrary is the Truth, and very great Advantages will be found by practiſing according to this Suppoſition. A conſtant Influx of the external Air, if it does not carry off ſome Part of the Spirit already generated, yet certainly catches up and diſſipates the fine, ſubtile, or oleaginous and ſaline Particles, whereof the Spirit is made, and thus conſiderably leſſens the Quantity. By a cloſe Fermentation this Inconveniency is avoided; all Air, except that included in the Veſſel, being excluded. The whole Secret conſiſts in leaving a moderate Space for

C 4 the

the Air at the Top of the Veſſel, unpoſſeſſed by the Liquor. When the Liquor is once fairly at work to bung it down cloſe, and thus ſuffer it to finiſh the Fermentation, without opening or giving it any more Vent than that afforded it by a proper Valve placed in the Caſk ; which, however is not of abſolute Neceſſity, when the empty Space, or rather that poſſeſſed by the Air, is about one tenth of the Gage ; the artificial Air, generated in the Operation being then ſeldom ſufficient to open a ſtrong Valve, or at moſt not to endanger the Caſk.

This Method may be practiſed to good Advantage by thoſe whoſe Buſineſs is not very large ; but it requires too much Time to be uſed by the large Dealers, who are in a manner forced to admit the free Air, and thus ſuſtain a conſiderable Loſs in their Quantity of Spirit, that the Fermentation may be finiſhed in the ſmall Time allowed for that Purpoſe. It may, however, be ſaid, that the ſilent, ſlow, and almoſt imperceptible vinous Fermentation, is univerſally the moſt perfect and advantageous.

During the whole Courſe of this Operation, the Veſſel ſhould be kept from all external Cold, or conſiderable Heat, in an equal, uniform, and moderate Temperature. In the Winter, a Stove Room, ſuch as is com-

mon

mon in *Germany*, would be very convenient for this Purpofe ; the Veffel being placed at a proper Diftance from the Stove : But at other Seafons no particular Apparatus is neceffary with us in *England*, if the Place allotted for the Bufinefs be but well defended from the Summer's Heat, and the ill Effects of cold bleak northern Winds.

The Operation is known to be perfected when the hiffing, or fmall bubbling Noife can be no longer heard, upon applying the Ear to the Veffel ; and alfo by the Liquor itfelf appearing clear to Eye, and having a pungent Sharpnefs on the Tongue. And that it may fully obtain thefe Properties, and be well fitted to yield a pure and perfectly vinous Spirit by Diftillation, it fhould be fuffered to ftand at reft in a fomewhat cooler Place, if practicable, than that in which it was fermented ; till it has thoroughly depofited and cleanfed itfelf of the grofs Lee, and become perfectly tranfparent, vinous and fragrant ; in which State it fhould be committed to the Still, and the Spirit obtained will not only exceed that obtained in the common Way in Quantity, but alfo in Fragrance, Pungency, and Vinofity.

C H A P.

CHAP. III.

Of Distillation in general.

HAVING in the two preceding Chapters laid down the best Methods of Brewing and Fermentation, we shall now proceed to the Method of Distillation.

And in order to lead our Readers methodically through the Path which lies before them, we shall begin with explaining the Principles of Distillation; or, the Method of extracting the spirituous Parts of Bodies.

To extract the Spirits is to cause such an Action by Heat, as to cause them to ascend in Vapour from the Bodies which detain them.

If this Heat be natural to Bodies, so that the Separation be made without any adventitious Means, it is called Fermentation, which we have already explained.

If it be produced by Fire, or other heating Power, in which the Alembic is placed, it is called Digestion, or Distillation: Digestion, if the Heat only prepares the Materials for the Distillation of their Spirits; and Distillation, where the Action is of
                                    sufficient

fufficient Efficacy to caufe them to afcend in
Vapour, and diftil.

This Heat is that which puts the infenfi-
ble Parts of a Body, whatever it be, into
Motion, divides them, and caufes a Paffage
for the Spirits inclofed herein, by difengag-
ing them from the Phlegm and the earthy
Particles by which they are inclofed.

Diftillation confidered in this Light, is not
unworthy the Attention and Countenance of
the Learned. This Art is of infinite Extent;
whatever the whole Earth produces, Flowers, Fruits, Seeds, Spices, aromatic and
vulnerary Plants, odoriferous Drugs, &c.
are its Objects, and come under its Cog-
nizance; but we generally confine it to Li-
quids of Tafte and Smell; and to the fimple and fpirituous Waters of aromatic and
vulnerary Plants. With regard to its Utility, we fhall omit faying any thing here,
as we fhall give fufficient Proofs of it in the
Sequel.

C H A P. IV.

Of particular Diftillation.

Diftillation is generally divided into three
Kinds; the firft is called Diftillation
per afcenfum, which is when the Fire, or
other

other Heat, applied to the Alembic, containing the Materials, cauſes the Spirits to
aſcend. This is the moſt common, and indeed almoſt the only kind uſed by Diſtillers.

The ſecond is called Diſtillation *per deſ-
cenſum*; which is, when the Fire being
placed upon the Veſſel precipitates, or cauſes
the Spirit to deſcend. This Kind is hardly
ever uſed by Diſtillers, but to obtain the
Eſſence or Oil of Cloves.

The third is termed Diſtillation *per latus*,
or oblique Diſtillation; but this being uſed
only by the Chemiſts we ſhall ſay nothing
farther of it here.

With regard to the different Methods of
Diſtillation, occaſioned by the different Veſſels, or Materials made uſe of to excite Heat,
improperly called Diſtillation; they are of
various Kinds, and ſhall be explained as
they occur in the Work.

There are various Kinds of Diſtillation,
ſome of which ariſe from the different Conſtructions of Alembics; ſuch are the Diſtillation by the common Alembic, with a
Refrigeratory, the Glaſs Alembic, the ſer-
pentine Alembic, and the Retort: Others
are produced from the Heat ſurrounding
the

the Alembic ; ſuch as the Diſtillation in *Balneum Mariæ*, the Vapor, the Sand, the Dung, and the Lime Baths.

Theſe different Methods of Diſtilling, we ſhall explain in enumerating the Operations in which they are moſt proper ; and proceed to treat of the different Forms of Alembics and ther Conſtructions.

CHAP. V.

Of ALEMBICS, *and their different Conſtructions.*

THE Alembic is a Veſſel uſually of Copper tined, which ſerves for, and is eſſential to all Operations in the Diſtillery.

There are ſeveral Sorts of Alembics, all different, either with regard to Matter or Form. As, the common Alembic with a Refrigeratory, the earthern and the glaſs Alembic, the *Balneum Mariæ*, and the Vapour-Bath Alembic.

Every one of theſe being of a different Conſtruction, are alſo uſed in different Operations,

The

The common Alembic confifts principally of two Parts, the lower Part called the Body, and the upper termed the Head.

The Body confifts of two Pieces, the lower called the Cucurbit, and the upper the Crown. The Curcubit, or lower Part of the Body, is a kind of Receptacle proportioned to the Size of the Alembic, in which the Bodies to be diftilled are placed.

The Crown, or upper Part of the Body, is alfo another Part of the Alembic; and is that Part of the Body to which the Head is immediately luted. But an Idea of thofe feveral Alembics will be much better attained from the following Figures, which reprefent them much ftronger to the Imagination than is poffible to be done by Words.

Fig. 1. Is a common Alembic, as it appears before it is placed in a Furnace, where *a* is the Bottom, *b* the Crown, *c* the Head.

Fig. 2. Is the Body without the Head; *a* the Rim or Top of the Crown where the Head is luted.

Fig. 3.

Fig. 3. The Head ; *a* the Rim where it is to be luted to the Body ; *b* the Nose, or End which is luted into the Worm.

Fig. 4. The Worm, as it appears when out of the Tub in which it is fixed when in use ; *a* the End into which the Still Head is inserted, *b* that which conveys the Liquor into the Receiver.

Fig 5. Two Stills at work in one Refrigeratory ; *a, b* the two Still Heads, *c, d* the Bodies inclosed in the Brick-Work ; *e, e* the two Fire-Places ; *f, f* the two Ash-Holes ; *g* a Common Receiver ; *b* a Spout Receiver, called by Chemists a Separating-Glass, used in the Distillation of Herbs, in order to extract their essential Oil ; *i* a Crane for drawing the Water out of the Refrigeratory.

Fig. 6. A small Still with a Refrigeratory ; *a* the Body, *b* the Head, *c* the Refrigeratory filled with Water, *d* the Receiver, luted to the Bec of the Alembic.

Fig. 7. A Glass Alembic to be used as a *Balneum Mariæ* ; *a* the Body, *b* the Head, *c* the Bec, which is to be luted to the Receiver, *d* a Trivet on which it is standing in the Water.

Fig.

Fig. 8. A proper Receiver for the Glaſs Alembic, called by Chemiſts a Bolt-Head, or Matraſs.

Fig 9. The Glaſs Alembic placed in a Copper Veſſel; *a* the Copper Veſſel filled with Water, *b* the Body of the Glaſs Alembic, *c* the Head, *d* the Receiver luted at *e* to the Bec of the Alembic.

Fig. 10. A cold Still for diſtilling ſimple Waters; *a* the Head, *b* the Bec, or Noſe, *c* the Receiver, *d* the Plate on which Herbs are laid.

Fig. 11. A Veſſel for Digeſtion, called by Chemiſts a Pelican or circulatory Veſſel; *a* the Body, *b* the Head, *c, c* two Tubes, luted at *d, d*, by which the Liquor returns from the Head into the Body; *e* a Furnace on which it is placed, *f* the Fire-place, *g* the Aſh-hole.

Fig. 12. Another Receiver, uſed when it is neceſſary to lute it to the End of the Worm, in order to prevent the moſt volatile Parts from being evaporated, and loſt.

CHAP.

CHAP. VI.

Of the ACCIDENTS *that too often happen in performing the Proceſſes of* DISTILIA-TION.

AMONG the Accidents which frequently happen in Diftilling, the leaft of all is for the Operation to mifcarry and the Ingredients to be loft.

And this being a Subject of the greateft Importance we fhall treat it with all poffible Accuracy.

All Accidents are occafioned by Fire, their primary Caufe; by want of Attention they get too much Head, and Fear often fuffers them to become irremediable.

The firft Accident which may happen by the Fire, is when a Diftiller, by too great a Heat, caufes the Ingredients to be burnt at the Bottom of the Still; by this Means his Liquor is fpoiled by an empereumatic Tafte, and the Tin is melted off from the Alembic. An Empereuma refembles the Smell of burnt Tobacco, and is produced in Liquors by too great a Degree of Heat. To illuftrate this, diftil any Fruit, Flowers, or any Aromatic whatever; but efpecially

D   fomething

something whose Smell is very volatile, draw off only the best, unlute the Alembic, and what remains in the Still, will be found to have a very disagreeable Smell; whence it follows, that if a little more had been drawn off, it would have spoiled what was before obtained.

If the Fire be too violent, the extraordinary Ebullition of the Contents causes them to ascend into the Head; and, if a Glass Alembic, they fall ignited into the Recipient; the Heat breaks it, the Spirits are dissipated, and often take Fire from the Heat of the Furnace.

If the Fire be too strong, the Bottom of the Still becomes red hot, the Materials inflamed, and consequently the Fire reaches the Recipient.

When an earthern Alembic is used, the closest Attention is requisite to keep the Fire from burning the Materials at the Bottom. The Head, which is always of Glass, bursts, and the Spirits are spilt, and often catch fire. And the Remedy becomes the more difficult, as Earth retains the Fire much longer than a common Alembic.

If the Alembic be not firmly fixed, it is soon put out of Order, falls down and un-
lutes

lutes itfelf; thus the Liquor is fpilt, and the Vapour fets the Spirits on fire.

If all the Joints be not carefully luted, the Spirits at their firft Effort iffue through the leaft Aperture, run into the Fire, which is propagated into the Alembic by the Vapour.

In Diftillations where the Phlegm afcends firft, its Humidity penetrates the Lute, and loofens it, fo that when the fpirituous Vapours afcend, they are expofed to the fame Accident.

Laftly, when the Recipient is unluted, efpecially if near full, without the greateft Circumfpection the Spirits will be fpilt, and fo catch Fire.

Hltherto I have only given a fimple Account of what daily happens to Diftillers; but the Confequences of thefe Accidents are infinitely more terrible than the Accidents themfelves; for an Artift to lofe his Time, his Labour and Goods, is no fmall Matter; but it follows from what we have premifed, that both his Life and Fortune are in danger from thefe Conflagrations. Inftances of the former are too common, as well as thofe of the latter, relating to the

Danger

Danger to which the Operator is exposed. They are evident, and we have seen very lately three Instances sufficient to intimidate the most sanguine. The Spirits catch, the Alembic and Recipient fly, and the inflamed Vapour becomes present Death to all who breathe it.

The Rectifiers, who perform the most dangerous Operations of Distillery, are particularly exposed to these terrible Accidents ; the Fineness of the Spirit at the same time that it renders it more inflammable, also causes the Fire to spread with the greater Rapidity. And when their Storehouses are once on fire, they are seldom or never saved.

Possibly I may be censured for my Concifeness on this Head ; indeed the Importance of it requires the most particular Discussion ; but intending to speak of the Methods proper to prevent these Accidents, I shall close this Chapter, with recommending the Subject of it to the serious Reflection of all concerned in Distillation. And it being hitherto omitted, though of all others it requires the Attention of the Distiller, I shall further observe, that these Operations should never be left to Servants. What can be expected from ignorant Persons ? Fear will

seize

ſeize them, when the greateſt Preſence of Mind is requiſite.——Let us now proceed to the Methods of preventing, or at leaſt leſſening their Effects.

CHAP. VII.

Of the Methods of preventing Accidents.

TO have informed the Reader of the Accidents which happen in Diſtilling, would have been of little Conſequence, without ſhewing, at the ſame Time, the Methods of preventing them. In order therefore to fortify him againſt the Terror, which the foregoing Chapter may have excited, we will here point out the Remedies for all the Caſes before ſpecified.

To prevent Accidents, two Things eſpecially muſt be known, and adverted to.

1. The Knowledge of the Fire, which depends on the Fuel, whether Wood or Coal.

2. The Manner of luting ſo as to prevent the Vapours from eſcaping through it, and by that Means of ſetting the whole on fire.

D 2   The

The hardeſt Wood generally makes the quickeſt Fire, ſuch as Beech, Oak, Holm, Elm, &c. The white Woods, as the Aſh, the Poplar, the Willow, and the Birch, make a milder Fire. This holds good alſo of the Coal made of theſe two kinds of Wood; and, conſequently, the Nature of the Wood or Coals muſt determine the Fire, and the Action of this muſt be proportioned to the Effect intended to be produced by it. That is, the Capacity of the Alembic, the Matters to be diſtilled, and their Quantity. The ſame may alſo be ſaid of Pit Coal, which is generally uſed in *England*.

It is evident, that the larger the Alembic, the more Fire is neceſſary. What has not been digeſted, alſo, requires more Fire than that which has been prepared by that Operation. Spices require a ſtronger Fire than Flowers; a Diſtillation of Simple Waters more than that of ſpirituous Liquors.

The ſureſt Way of aſcertaining the neceſſary Degree of Fire, is to regulate it by the Materials, as they are more or leſs diſpoſed to yield them Spirits, &c. and this is done as follows. The Operator muſt not leave the Alembic, but attentively liſten to what paſſes within, when the Fire begins to heat it. When the Ebulition

lition becomes too vehement, the Fire muſt be leſſened, either by taking out ſome of the Fuel, or covering it with Aſhes or Sand.

It requires a long Experience in the ſeveral Caſes, before a Diſtiller can acquire a competent Knowledge in this important Point. Nor is it poſſible to determine the Degree of Fire from the Quantity of Fuel ; Judgment, aſſiſted by Experience, muſt ſupply this Defect.

Every thing being determined with regard to the Degree of Fire, we ſhall now proceed to explain the Method of luting Alembics.

By the Term luting an Alembic, we mean, the cloſing the Joints through which the Spirits might tranſpire.

Lute is a Compoſition of common Aſhes, well ſifted, and ſoaked in Water ; Clay, and a kind of Paſte made of Meal or Starch are alſo uſed for this Purpoſe ; which, as I before obſerved, is to cloſe all the Joints, &c. in order to confine the Spirits from tranſpiring.

Good Luting is one of the ſureſt Methods of preventing Accidents. An Alembic, where all Tranfpiration is prevented, having nothing to fear but the too great Fiercenefs of the Fire ; and that may be regulated by the Rules already laid down.

The refrigerating Alembic is moftly ufed. The Body and the Head are joined to each other ; but notwithftanding the greateft Care be taken in luting the Juncture, there will ftill be fome imperceptable Interftice for Tranfpiration ; and the leaft being of the greateft Confequence, a Piece of ftrong Paper, fhould be pafted over the Joint, and the Alembic never left, till the Spirits begin to flow into the Receiver, in order to apply frefh Paper, if the former fhould contract any Moifture. The Mafter himfelf fhould carefully attend to this, and whatever Precaution may have been previoufly ufed, the Eye muft be conftantly upon it.

The Alembic, when vinous Spirits are diftilled, fhould be luted with Clay, carefully fpread round the Junctures, in order to prevent all Tranfpiration ; becaufe the Confequences here are terrible ; for when the Fire catches a large Quantity, it is often irremediable. Befides, as this Earth cracks in drying, it muft be often moiftened, and frefh applied, on the firft Appearance of any Occafion for it.

The

The Retort is alſo luted with Clay ; but as glaſs Retorts are alſo uſed, they are often coated with the ſame Clay, to prevent their melting by the Intenſeneſs of the Fire.

. Laſtly, the earthern and glaſs Alembics are luted with Paper and Paſte as above.—— Having thus explained the great Conſequence of Circumſpection with regard to Luting, and the Degree of Fire, we ſhall now proceed to a third Method of preventing them, and cloſe this Chapter with a ſhort Obſervation on portable Furnaces ; which is, That Alembics being never thoroughly ſecure on this kind of Furnaces, a Hook ſhould be faſtened to the Refrigerant for fixing it to the Wall.

C H A P. VIII.

Of the Remedies for Accidents, when they happen.

NOtwithſtanding the beſt of Rules, and the ſtricteſt Obſervation, it is impoſſible entirely to prevent Accidents, and therefore it is of no leſs Importance to point out the Remedies on thoſe Occaſions.

The moſt eſſential, are Courage and Preſence of Mind ; Fear only increaſing the Misfortune.　　　　　　　1. If

1. If the Fire be too violent it muſt be covered, but not ſo as totally to prevent its Action, as by that Means the Proceſs of the Diſtillation would be interrupted, and render it more difficult and leſs perfect.

2. When the Ingredients burn, which you will ſoon diſcover by the Smell, the Fire muſt be immediately put out, in order to prevent the whole Charge of the Still being entirely ſpoiled, which would otherwiſe inevitably be the Conſequence.

3. If the Spirits ſhould catch fire, the firſt care is to unlute immediately the Receiver, and ſtop both the End of the Beak and Mouth of the Receiver with wet Clothes.

The Fire muſt then be put out, and if the Flame iſſued through the Luting, the Joints muſt be cloſed with a wet Cloth, which, together with Water, ſhould never be wanting in a Diſtil-houſe.

4. If the Alembic be of Earth, and the Contents burn at the Bottom, the Fire muſt immediately be put out, the Alembic removed, and Water thrown upon it, till the Danger is over; and, for farther Security, covered with a wet Cloth.

5. If

5. If after all your Care in cloſing the Junctures to prevent Tranſpiration, you perceive any thing amiſs, while the Spirits are aſcending, apply Clay, or any other Compoſition, in order to ſtop the Aperture, and have always a wet Cloth ready to ſtifle the Flame, if the Spirits ſhould take fire.

6. If the Heat detaches the Lute, or it becomes moiſt, immediately apply another, having always ready what is neceſſary for performing it. Should the Tranſpiration be ſo violent, that you cannot immediately apply a freſh Lute, clap a wet Cloth round the Joint, and keep it on firm and tight, till the Spirits have taken their Courſe. But if notwithſtanding all your Efforts the Tranſpiration ſhould increaſe, ſo that you fear a Conflagration, remove the Receiver as ſoon as poſſible from the Fire, and afterwards your Alembic, if portable; but if otherwiſe, put out the Fire immediately.

7. The Charge being worked off, be cautious in luting the Receiver, that nothing be ſpilt on the Furnace, and carry it to ſome Diſtance from it, that the Spirits exhaling may not take fire.

8. Laſtly obſerve, that wherever a Remedy is required, there muſt be no Candle uſed;

used; for the spirituous Vapours easily take Fire, and propagate the Flame to the Vessels from whence they issue.

All that has been hitherto said concerns only the Management of the Alembic; but what remains is still more interesting, and relates to those who work it, that they may not, by conquering the Accident, destroy themselves.

On discovering any of the above Accidents, when the Flame has not yet reached the Spirits, let the Remedies already mentioned be applied, either with regard to the Lute, or the Violence of the Fire.

But if the Flame has reached the Alembic, the following Precautions are to be used.

The Operator must not approach the Alembic without a wet Cloth over his Mouth and Nostrils, it being immediate Death to inhale the inflamed Vapour.

In hastening to stop any Accident, be careful to approach the Side opposite to that whither the Air impels the Flame; for, without this Precaution you would be involved in it, and could not, without the utmost Difficulty, extricate yourself from it.

If

If notwithftanding this Precaution, the Eddy of the Air fhould force the Flame to your Side, quit the Place immediately, and do not return till its Direction be changed, always taking care to have a wet linen Cloth before your Nofe and Mouth, and keep your-felf on the Side oppofite to the Direction of the Flame : And alfo to have another fuch Cloth, in order to fmother the Flame, and clofe the Crevife through which the Spirits iffue.

Should it be your Misfortune to be co-vered with inflamed Spirits, wrap yourfelf in a wet Sheet, which fhould be always ready for that Purpofe. Self-Prefervation is of too great Importance that any of thefe Precautions fhould be omitted in fuch Va-riety of Dangers.

If the Fire has acquired fuch a Head that it cannot be ftopt, the Receiver muft be broke, and the Alembic, if portable, thrown down ; but no Perfon muft be fuf-fered to go near them, efpecially thofe who are Strangers to the Bufinefs.

In a defperate Cafe, like that of a large Quantity of rectified Spirit taking Fire, if Time permit, the Communication of the Beak of the Alembic with the Recipient, which is ufually a Cafk, muft be cut off, by

closely

clofely ftopping the Bung ; and be fure no Candle come near the Receiver, leaving the reft, as the Danger would be too great to expofe ones felf to the Flames of a large Charge, and the Diftiller's Safety fhould be principally confidered.

I thought it my Duty to give my Reader thefe Informations, and hope that in the Practice of Diftillation, he will find them of great Advantage.

C H A P. IX.

On the Necefity of often cooling the Alembic, as another Means of preventing Accidents.

THE Refrigerant is fo effential a Part of the Alembic, that for want of it feveral other Expedients are made ufe of to perform its Office, for cooling thofe whofe Capacity, Brittlenefs, or laftly the Conftruction, will not admit of their having any.

The Refrigerant is ufually in proportion to the Capacity of the Alembic, for which the following may ferve as a Rule, that the Capacity of the Refrigerant fhould be to that of the Alembic, as 14 to 8.

The Necefity of cooling the Head of the Alembic is felf-evident to all who have
the

the least Knowledge of Distillation, as it condenses the Spirits, cools them, and causes them to flow into the Receiver, which, if of Glass, would otherwise be broken by the Heat; and consequently serves to prevent Conflagrations.

The Alembics of the *Balneum Mariæ*, and the Vapour Bath, ought also to have Refrigerants, like the common Alembic, unless they are of Glass.

Those of Earth and Glass are cooled, as we have already observed, with a wet Cloth, which is also used to cool the Head of other kinds of Alembics. But it is not difficult to contrive one which may be placed in a Refrigerant; such as the following.

To a common small Still apply and lute a Worm, or long tin or pewter Tube, forming several Circumvolutions, of the same Circumference with the Body, in order to give it some Elevation, place this Worm in a Refrigerant, proportioned to the Alembic. If the Capacity of this Alembic should make it bear too much on the Neck of the Matrass, it may be supported by a Trevit of the same Circumference as the Body itself: The Extremity of the Worm may have a Beak projecting beyond the Side of the Refrigerant, for conveying the Spirits into the Receiver.

This

This Apparatus will be attended with little Expence, will save the Diftiller the Trouble of being perpetually cooling the Head of the Alembic, and is such a Safe-guard againft Accidents, that if the Worm be well luted, nothing need be apprehended but from the Violence of the Fire.

This Method of Practice, therefore, is productive of three valuable Particulars: The firft is, that by cooling the Spirits it preferves the Receiver, and obviates the Accidents arifing from their Heat. The second is, that the Spirits being kept in a moderate Heat, the Tranfpiration is lefs, and confequently the Spirits procured by the Operation have more Tafte, Smell and Fragrancy than they would otherwife have had.

Experience demonftrates, that when the Spirits flow hot into the Receiver, however attentive the Diftiller may be to lute the Junctures of the Alembic, there will be a very fenfible Evaporation, which even in fimple Waters greatly depreciates the Goodnefs of the Liquor.

Laftly, the third is, that the Cooling of Alembics is what principally contributes to the Perfection of the Operation ; becaufe the

the Coolneſs of the Head precipitates the Phlegm, and in the Caſe of too great a Degree of Fire, and where the Ebullition is too vehement, if after taking away Part of the Fire, or covering it, the Ebullition ſhould continue, the Head may be cooled with a wet Cloth, till the Ebullition is reduced.

As there is a Neceſſity of cooling the Alembic; ſo what we have ſaid cannot be too carefully obſerved. In fine, the Contraſt of Cold and Heat, equally concurring, but by Methods directly oppoſite, to the ſame Proceſs, and the Perfection of the Diſtillation, is a Phœnomenon, which deſerves the Attention of all who ſtudy the Operations of Nature.

C H A P. X.

Of the Neceſſity of putting Water into the Alembic, for ſeveral Diſtillations.

TWO principal Advantages attend putting Water into the Alembic. The firſt is, to prevent the Loſs the Diſtiller would incur without that Precaution, and ſo prevent any Alteration in the Liquor procured by Diſtillation. This we ſhall illuſtrate by an Example. Suppoſe a Diſtiller ſhould attempt to rectify Spirits of Wine, without putting Water in the Alembic. It

E

is evident, that the Fire will confume Part of it, which is entirely lofs, becaufe the fame Quantity of Spirit cannot be procured from it, which might, had there been any thing to moderate the Action of the Fire, which now preyed upon it.

Secondly, If Liquors are impregnated with ftrong Ingredients, efpecially Seeds, and the Quantity be fufficient to abforb all the Phlegm, a great Quantity of Spirit muft be left in the Still, or the Ingredients will burn, and the Spirits contract an empreumatic Tafte, which is the more detrimental to the Spirit, as it is increafed by Age.

Thirdly, If no Water be put into the Alembic with the Ingredients, the Spirit will be rendered finer by them, and the Fire, if ever fo little too ftrong, will caufe the Ingredients to burn, and the Spirits to contract an Empyreuma ; a Misfortune eafily prevented by this Precaution.

Thus it is a Safe-guard againft Accidents : But befides, Water being mixed with the Ingredients, they are at once prevented from burning, and the Spirit not weakened ; for no fooner are the Ingredients put in Motion by the Fire, than the Spirits immediately afcend, and the Liquor lofes nothing of its Quality, provided the Receiver be removed as foon as the Phelegm begins to afcend.

The

The Water therefore prevents the Wafte of the Spirits, and thus the Diftiller lofes nothing of his Goods ; whereas, without Water, the Spirits by impregnating the Materials, their Quantity muft be lefs. With regard to the Phlegm, there is no Difficulty in finding when it begins to afcend, the firft Drop being cloudy, and when it has continued dropping for fome time, it is perceived by a milky Caft at the Bottom of the Receiver.

Laftly, The Diftiller is no Lofer with regard to the Quality of his Liquor, which is not at all weakened thereby. Thus it is attended with the two capital Advantages, the Profit of the Diftiller, and the Perfection of the Liquor. Let us now proceed to the different Manners of Diftillation.

C H A P. XI.

Of the particular Advantages attending every kind of Diftillation.

IN the third Chapter we mentioned the feveral kinds of Diftillation, we fhall here enlarge on the particular Advantages of each, and in what Circumftances each is to be ufed.

In

In order for Diftillation, the Alembic muft be charged with Materials, and placed on a Fire, or Subftances capable of producing the fame Effect.

The Method of Diftilling with the common refrigerant Alembic.

This Method of Diftilling is the moft generally ufed, being one of the moft fpeedy and profitable, as it requires fewer Preparatives, and lefs Time.

To diftil with the common Alembic, the Body of it muft be thoroughly cleanfed, that no Tafte or Smell of any preceding Materials may remain. The Materials are then to be put into the Alembic; but care muft be taken that the Alembic be not above half full, in order that the Materials may have fufficient Room to move, without choaking the Neck of the Alembic. The fame Care muft be taken with regard to the Head, it muft be thoroughly cleanfed and dried; for it often happens that fome fmall Quantity of Water is left in the Rim, which renders the firft Spirits foul, and, by endeavouring to feparate it from the other, fome, and that the moft volatile Part of the Spirit, will be loft.

After

After this the two Parts of the Alembic are to be carefully luted with ſtrong brown. Paper, well paſted on, and the Noſe of the Alembic luted to the Worm; after which the Fire ſhould be immediately made under the Still, leſt too long an Infuſion ſhould prejudice the Liquor.

This Alembic being worked on an open Fire, the Operation is quicker than any other; but the Degree of Fire requires a very cloſe Attention; as a different Management is neceſſary to different Materials. The Water of the Refrigeratory muſt be changed from time to time, and if the Caſe requires it, the whole Head, but eſpecially the Bec, muſt be kept cold.

Of Diſtillation in Sand, and in what Caſes it ſhould be uſed.

This Species of Diſtillation is performed in two different Manners. Firſt, by covering the Fire with Sand or Aſhes, and placing the Alembic upon it. This Method is very neceſſary in Digeſtion, and for the perfect Rectification of Spirits. Sand is abſolutely neceſſary for moderating the Action of the Fire, when there is Reaſon to fear the Matter contained in the Bottom of the Alembic will burn.

E 3 The

The second Method of Sand Diſtillation, is to take the fineſt River Sand, and after thoroughly waſhing it, put into the Alembic a Quantity ſufficient to cover it three Fingers deep; after which the Still is to be charged with the Ingredients to be diſtilled. This ſerves inſtead of Water in certain Caſes, where the Uſe of it would prejudice the Ingredients; as in the fine ſpirituous Waters impregnated with the aromatic Parts of Flowers; the Sand preventing the Ingredients from burning. It is alſo neceſſary in diſtilling rectified Spirits from Seeds.

This Operation being finiſhed, the Alembic muſt be thoroughly cleanſed from the Sand, that the Taſte or Smell contained therein, be not communicated to any other Charge of different Ingredients.

Of Diſtilling in Balneum Mariæ, *and its Advantages.*

This Method of Diſtillation is of great Uſe in ſeveral Caſes. Its Operation is more perfect, and is ſubject to few, if any of thoſe Accidents attending Diſtillations on an open Fire.

In diſtilling ſweet-ſcented Waters from Flowers, aromatic Plants, and others of that

that kind, where neither Water, nor Spirit ought to be mixed with them, there is an abfolute Neceffity for ufing the *Balneum Mariæ* ; as by every other Diftillation, on an open Fire, the Ingredients would infallibly burn.

If Sand fhould be made ufe of, the Fire would melt the Tin from the Alembic, and the Contents be in the utmoft Danger of being burnt.

In diftilling in *Balneum Mariæ*, a glafs Alembic is generally ufed. This Alembic is to be placed in a Copper Veffel filled with Water. This Veffel ought at leaft to be of half the Height of the Alembic : at the Bottom of the Copper Veffel muft be a Trivet on which the Alembic is to be placed, that it may not touch the Bottom of the Copper, becaufe when the Water begins to boil, it difperfes itfelf towards the Sides, and leaving the Bottom dry, the Ingredients would be in danger of burning.

The Ufe of the *Balneum Mariæ* is excellent for thofe Ingredients which require little Spirit ; but if a Copper Alembic be ufed, be fure to place Sand at the Bottom, that the diftilled Liquor may not contract any ill Tafte or Smell. This Method is alfo advifeable in the Rectification of Spirits, on Account of the Danger attending this Operation when performed on a naked Fire.

Were this Method of Distillation as expeditious as that performed on a naked Fire, no other ought to be used; because it is subject to no Accidents, and at the same Time the Spirit, &c. distilled is much more fragrant and grateful.

In what Cases glass, or earthen Alembics are to be used; their Advantages and Disadvantages.

In the Chapter relating to Accidents, we have mentioned the earthen Alembic; we must now add, that it ought never to be used, except the Matter to be distilled have a-strong and bad Smell, and then seldom above once, unless it be for Ingredients of the same or similar Qualities.

This Alembic being very difficult to be managed, we can only recommend it in the Case above-mentioned.

As a naked Fire is generally applied to this Alembic, it requires a Furnace where the Fire may be gradually increased, on account of the Accidents to which it is liable.

The

The glaſs Alembic is more eaſily managed, as it is generally placed in a *Balneum Mariæ.* Its principal Uſe is for diſtilling Waters from Flowers, and making Quinteſſences; and were it not for the Length of the Operation, it would be preferable to any other Method.

This Alembic hardly admitting of a Refrigerant, a wet linen Cloth muſt be placed on the Head, and often changed.

The Receiver of this Alembic muſt not be very large, becauſe of the Fragility of the Bec; but if it were ever ſo little bent into a Curve, the Largeneſs of the Receiver would be of no Prejudice; becauſe then its whole Weight would be ſupported by its Stand.

Advantages of Diſtillation performed by the Vapour Bath.

This Method differs very little from the *Balneum Mariæ,* and is uſed nearly in the ſame Circumſtances; but has greatly the Advantage of the *Balneum Mariæ* in the Quickneſs of the Operation. And *Lemery,* in the firſt Part of his Courſe of Chemiſtry, affirms its Operation to be more perfect.

However

However that be, its Use is equal to that of the *Balneum Mariæ*; but in diftilling fweet-fcented Waters, or Flowers, Sand muſt be placed at the Bottom, that the Liquor may not contract a Taſte from the Copper.

Caſes where Dung, Husks of Grapes, and Lime, are to be uſed.

Theſe Subſtances are rarely uſed except in Digeſtions; and therefore of no great Uſe to Diſtillers, they uſing only hot Aſhes, or a Fire well covered for that Purpoſe.

If Dung be uſed it muſt be of the hotteſt kind, *viz.* that of the Horfe or Sheep, and the Quantity proportioned to the Heat intended. The Lime muſt be quick; and if the Heat required be moderate, Lime which has lain ſome time in the Air muſt be uſed. The ſame is to be obſerved with regard to the Huſks of Grapes. But in whatever manner theſe are uſed, the Digeſtions muſt be performed in a cloſe covered Veſſel.

CHAP.

C H A P. XII.

Of Bodies proper for Diftillation.

THIS Chapter alone might make a Volume, were we to make a particular Enumeration of all its Parts; but, as we have already obferved, we fhall confine ourfelves to the Diftillation of fimple and compound Waters, &c.

If we acquit ourfelves to the Satisfaction of the Public, we fhall enjoy the Pleafure of having treated of one Part entirely new; and, indeed, the only one that has been overlooked.

The Bodies proper for Diftillation, are Flowers, Fruits, Seeds, Spices and aromatic Plants.

By Diftillation and Digeftion, we extract the Colour and Smell of Flowers in fimple Waters and Effences.

We extract from Fruits, at leaft from fome, Colour, Tafte, &c.

From aromatic Plants, the Diftiller draws Spirits, Effences, fimple and compound Waters.

From

From Spices are procured Eſſences, or in the Language of the Chemiſts, Oils, and Perfumes, and alſo pure Spirits.

From Seeds or Berries are drawn ſimple Waters, pure Spirits; and from ſome, as thoſe of Aniſe, Fennel, and Juniper, Oil.

The Colour of Flowers is extracted by Infuſion, and likewiſe by Digeſtion in Brandy or Spirit of Wine: The Smell is extracted by Diſtillation; the ſimple Water with Brandy or Spirit of Wine.

What is extracted of the Colour of Flowers, by Infuſion in Water by a gentle Heat, or by Digeſtion in Brandy or Spirits of Wine, is called, in the Diſtiller's Phraſe, Tincture of Flowers.

The Colour of Fruits is extracted in the ſame manner, either by Infuſion or Digeſtion: Their Taſte is alſo procured by the ſame Proceſſes. But let it be obſerved, that the Time of theſe Operations muſt be limited; for otherwiſe the Fruit, after Fermentation, would render it acid. The Taſte is alſo extracted by Diſtillation in Spirit of Wine.

From aromatic Plants are extracted by the Alembic pure Spirits, Odours, and ſimple
ple

ple Waters. But thefe require different Methods of Diftillation. The firft by Water or Brandy only, the fecond by rectified Spirit, which will give them the greateft Excellency they are capable of.

The Plants themfelves with their Flowers may alfo be diftilled, which is ftill better.

From Spices are drawn Spirits, and oily or fpirituous Quinteffences. The Spirits are drawn by Brandy, or Spirit of Wine, with very little Water : The Oils are diftilled *per Defcenfum*; and the fpirituous Quinteffences by pounding the Spices, and after infufing them in Spirit of Wine, decanting it gently by Inclination.

From Seeds are extracted fimple Waters, Spirits and Oils. Very few of the firft and laft, Spirits being what is generally extracted from Seeds and Berries.

Some Diftillers, through a Notion of Frugality, diftil Seeds with Water ; but their Liquors are not to be compared with thofe which are diftilled with Spirits. When Oils are drawn from Seeds, the Operation is performed either by the *Balneum Mariæ*, or the Vapour Bath.

We

We only deliver in this Place, the firſt Elements of each of theſe Operations, which will be farther illuſtrated in the Sequel, when we treat more particularly of theſe Subjects.

C H A P. XIII.

Of what is procured by Diſtillation.

BY Diſtillation are procured Spirit, Eſſence, ſimple Waters and Phlegm.

Spirits are very difficult to be defined. I conſider them as the moſt ſubtil and volatile Parts of a Body.

All Bodies without Exception have Spirits more or leſs.

Theſe Parts are an ignited Subſtance, and conſequently by their own Nature diſpoſed to a violent Motion.

Theſe volatile Particles are more or leſs diſpoſed to ſeparate themſelves, as the Bodies are more or leſs porous, or abound with a greater or leſſer Quantity of Oil.

By the Term *Eſſence*, we underſtand the oleaginous Parts of a Body. An eſſential

Oil

Oil is found in all Bodies, being one of their conftituent Principles. I · have obferved in all my Diftillations, Spirit of Wine excepted, a foft unctuous Subftance floating on the Phlegm; and this Subftance is Oil, which we call Effence; and this is what we endeavour to extract.

Simple Waters are thofe diftilled from Plants, Flowers, &c. without the Help of Water, Brandy, or Spirit of Wine. Thefe Waters are commonly odoriferous, containing the Odour of the Body from whence it is extracted, and even exceeds in Smell the Body itfelf.

Phlegm is the aqueous Particles of Bodies; but whether an active or paffive Principle, we fhall leave to the Decifion of Chemifts.

It is of the laft Importance to a Diftiller to be well acquainted with its Nature; many miftaking for Phlegm feveral white and clouded Drops, which firft fall into the Receiver, when the Still begins to work. Thefe, however, are often the moft fpirituous Particles of the Matter in the Alembic, and confequently ought to be preferved. What has given occafion to this Miftake, is fome Humidity remaining in the Head, &c. of the Alembic. And had it been thoroughly wiped, the firft Drops would have been.

been equally bright with any during the whole Operation.

The following Remark deserves Attention. In Bodies that have been digested the Spirits ascend first; whereas in Charges not digested, the Phlegm ascends before the Spirits. The Reason of this is very plain and natural.

In Substances previously digested, the Action of the Fire no sooner causes the Matter in the Alembic to boil, than the Spirits, being the most volatile Parts, detach themselves, and ascend into the Head of the Alembic. But when the Matter to be distilled has not undergone a proper Digestion, the Spirits being intangled in the Phlegm, are less disposed to ascend, till the Phlegm itself separates, and gives them room to fly upward. The Phlegm being aqueous rises first: This is more particularly observable in Spices. I am, however, inclined to believe, that were the Operation performed in an Alembic, whose Head was at a great Distance from the Surface of the Charge, they would not ascend high enough to come over the Helm, but fall back again by their own Gravity, and by that means leave the Spirits at Liberty to ascend. But in the common Refrigatory Alembic this always happens.

If

If this Obfervation be not readily admitted, I appeal to Experience, which I defire
may be the Teft of every thing I fhall advance.

Another Obfervation, which has verified
the above Affertion by innumerable Inftances,
is, that in an extraordinary Run of Bufinefs,
when I had not time fufficient to digeft the
Subftances, I ufed to bruife them in a Mortar ; but notwithftanding the Trituration,
the Phlegm firft came over, and afterwards
the Spirits. But I defire to be underftood,
that I fpeak here only of the volatile Parts
of the Plants not drawn with vinous Spirits,
but contained in a fimple Water.

Another Remark I muft add, and which
I hope will be acceptable to the Curious,
as it has not yet been made public, though
doubtlefs the Obfervation has often occurred
to others ; it is this : That in mixed Charges,
confifting of Flowers, Fruits, and aromatic
Plants, put into the Alembic without a previous Digeftion, the Spirits of the Flowers
afcend firft ; and notwithftanding the Mixture, they contracted nothing of the Smell
or Tafte of the Fruits and Plants. Next
after the Spirits of the Flowers, thofe of the
Fruits afcend, not in the leaft impregnated
with the Smell or Tafte of either of the

F

Flowers

Flowers or Plants. And in the laſt Place the Spirits of the Plants diſtil no leſs neat than the former. Should this appear ſtrange to any one, Experience will convince him of the Truth.

Another Obſervation I have made on aromatic Herbs, is, that whether they are, or are not digeſted; whether the Spirits or Phlegm aſcend firſt; the Spirits contain very little of the Taſte and Smell of the Plants from whence they were extracted; and I have always been obliged to put to theſe Spirits a greater or leſſer Quantity of the Phlegm, in order to give the Spirits I had drawn the Taſte of an aromatic Odour of the Plants; the Phlegm containing the greateſt Quantity of both.

This Obſervation I inſert as of great Uſe to thoſe who practiſe Diſtillation.

As the Term Digeſtion often occurs in this Eſſay, I cannot avoid pointing out its Advantages, and even ſhew the Neceſſity of uſing it in ſeveral Circumſtances.

Subſtances are ſaid to be in Digeſtion, when they are infuſed in a Menſtruum, over a very ſlow Fire. This Preparation is often neceſſary in Diſtillation; for it tends to open the Bodies, and thereby free the Spirits.

rits from their Confinements, whereby they are the better enabled to aſcend.

Cold Digeſtions are the beſt; thoſe made by Fire, or in hot Materials, diminiſh the Quality of the Goods, as ſome Part, as the moſt volatile, will be loſt.

In order to procure Eſſences, the Bodies muſt be prepared by Digeſtion. It is even of abſolute Neceſſity for extracting the Spirits and Eſſences of Spices.

C H A P. XIV.

Of the proper Seaſon for Diſtilling.

FLOWERS of all Kinds muſt be diſtilled in their proper Seaſons. To begin with the Violet. Its Colour and Smell can only be extracted when it is in its greateſt Vigour, which is not at its firſt Appearance, nor when it begins to decay. *April* is the Month in which it is in its greateſt Perfection ; the Seaſon being never ſo forward in *March*, as to give the Violet its whole Fragrancy.

The ſame muſt be obſerved of all other Flowers. And let them be gathered at the hotteſt Time of the Day ; the Odour and

Fra-

Fragrancy of Flowers being then in their greateſt Perfection.

The ſame Obſervation holds good, with regard to Fruits; to which muſt be added, that they are the fineſt, and of the moſt beautiful Colour, eſpecially thoſe from whence Tinctures are drawn; they muſt be free from all Defects, as the Goods would by that Means be greatly detrimented.

Berries and Aromatics may be diſtilled at any Seaſon, all that is neceſſary being a good Choice. But in this Diſtillers are ſometimes miſtaken, as may eaſily happen without a very accurate Knowledge. We ſhall therefore, in the Sequel, lay down more particular Directions for making a proper Choice of Materials.

C H A P. XV.

Of the Filtration of Liquors.

Filtration conſiſts in paſſing Liquors thro' ſome porous Subſtance, in order to free them from thoſe Particles which obſcure their Brightneſs.

Nothing is finer than a Liquor newly diſtilled; but the Syrup and colouring Particles

ticles render it thick and opaque ; in order, therefore, to reſtore their Brightneſs they are filtrated, which is done by paſſing them through Sand, Paper, Cloth, &c.

All the Attention of the Diſtiller cannot in ordinary Operations always prevent ſome aqueous Particles from riſing with the Spirits, either in the Beginning of the Proceſs, in thoſe Compoſitions where they aſcend firſt, or at the Concluſion when they riſe laſt. As this is almoſt unavoidable, ſo it is alſo ſometimes neceſſary.

In diſtilling Flowers, or aromatic Plants, freſh gathered, the Phlegm riſes firſt ; and this Part cannot be taken out of the Receiver without depriving the Spirits of a conſiderable Part of their Fragrancy.

In diſtilling Spices, their Odour being more entangled, will remain in the Alembic till Part of the Phlegm is drawn off. But when, inſtead of theſe Subſtances, their Quinteſſences are uſed, the Neceſſity ceaſes. But the Phlegm commonly cauſing a Cloudineſs in the Liquor, it may be rendered tolerably fine, by pouring it gently off by Inclination, without the Trouble of Filtratration, the aqueous Particles, by their Gravity, falling to the Bottom. But to render it entirely bright and fine, put ſome Cot-

F 3 ton

ton in a Funnel, and pour the Liquor thro'
it, by which means the aqueous Particles
will be retained in the Cotton. You muſt
however remember to cover the Top of
the Funnel, to prevent the moſt volatile
Parts of the Spirits from evaporating.

CHAP. XVI.

Of the Diſtillation of Malt Spirits.

THE Waſh, or Liquor being prepared
by Brewing and Fermentation, as directed in the firſt and ſecond Chapters of
this Treatiſe, the Still is to be charged with
it, and worked off with a pretty briſk Fire.
But it ſhould be obſerved, that the only Apparatus uſed in this Proceſs, is the Alembic with a Refrigeratory, as repreſented in
Fig. 1.

The Waſh being of a mucilaginous Nature, a particular Management is neceſſary
to prevent its burning, and cauſe it to work
kindly in the Still : If it ſhould happen to be
burnt in the Operation, the Spirit will have a
moſt diſagreeable Flavour, which can hardly
ever be removed ; and therefore to prevent
this ill Effect, the Waſh ſhould be made
dilute or thin, the Fire well regulated, and
the whole kept in a continual Agitation
during the whole Proceſs. The moſt judi-
cious

cious Diftillers always take care to have
their Waſh ſufficiently diluted, and con-
ſtantly find their Spirit the purer for it.
With regard to the Fire, it may be eaſily
kept regular by a conſtant Attendance, and
obſerving never to ſtir it haſtily, or throw
on freſh Fuel; and the ſtirring of the Liquor in the Still is to be effected by Means
of a Paddle, or Bar kept in the Liquor till it
juſt begins to boil, which is the Time for
luting on the Head; and after which there
is no great Danger, but from the improper
Management of the Fire: This is the common Way; but it is no eaſy Matter to hit the
exact Time, and the doing it either too late, or
too ſoon, is attended with great Inconvenience, ſo that ſeveral have diſcovered other
Methods; ſome put more ſolid Bodies into the
the Still with the Waſh; others place ſome
proper Matter at the Bottom and Sides of
the Still, which are the Places where the
Fire acts with the greateſt Force.

The Uſe of the Paddle would, however,
anſwer better than either of theſe Methods,
could it be continued during the whole
Time the Still is working; and this may be
done by the following Method: Let a ſhort
Tube of Iron or Copper be ſoldered in the
Center of the Still-head, and let a croſs Bar
be placed below in the ſame Head, with a
Hole in the Middle, correſponding to that

at the Top ; through both these let an iron Pipe be carried down in the Still, and let an iron Rod be passed through this with wooden Sweeps at its End ; this Rod may be continually worked by a Winch at the Stillhead, and the Sweeps will continually keep the Bottom and Sides scraped clean, the Interstices of the Tube being all the time well crammed with Tow to prevent any Evaporation of the Spirit.

The same Effect may, in a great Measure, be produced by a less laborious Method, namely, by placing a Parcel of cylindrical Sticks lengthways, so as to cover the whole Bottom of the Still, or by throwing in a loose Parcel of Faggot Sticks at a Venture ; for the Action of the Fire below moving the Liquor, at the same time gives Motion to the Sticks, making them act continually like a Parcel of Stirrers upon the Bottom and Sides of the Still, which might, if necessary, be furnished with Buttons and Loops, to prevent them from starting. Some also use a Parcel of fine Hay laid upon the loose Sticks; and secured down by two cross Poles, laid from Side to Side, and in the same Manner fastened down with Loops. Care is to be taken in this Case not to press the Hay against the Sides of the Still; for that would scorch nearly as soon as the Wash itself ; but the Sticks never will: These are simple

but

but effectual Contrivances, and in point of Elegance, they may be improved at Pleafure.

There is another Inconvenience attending the diftilling of Malt Spirit, which is, when all the Bottoms, or grofs mealy Fœculence is put into the Still along with the Liquor, the thinner Part of the Wafh going off in Form of Spirit; the mealy Mafs grows by Degrees more and more ftiff, fo as to fcorch towards the latter Part of the Operation. The beft Method of remedying this is to have a Pipe with a Stop-cock, leading from the upper Part of the Worm-tub into the Still; fo that upon a half, or a quarter Turn, it may continually fupply a little Stream of hot Water, in the fame Proportion as the Spirit runs off, by which Means the Danger of fcorching is avoided, and the Operation, at the fame time, not in the leaft retarded.

In *Holland*, the Malt Diftillers work all their Wafh thick, with the whole Body of Meal among it; yet they are fo careful in keeping their Stills clean, and fo regular and nice in the Management of their Fires, that though they ufe no Artifice at all on this Head, only to charge the Still while it is hot and moift, they very rarely have the Misfortune to fcorch, except now and then

in

in the Depth of Winter.   When ſuch an Accident has once happened in a Still, they are extremely careful to ſcrape, ſcrub and ſcour off the Remains of the burnt Matter, otherwiſe they find the ſame Accident very liable to happen again in the ſame Place. But beyond all the other Methods in Uſe on this Occaſion, would be the working the Stills not by a dry Heat, but in a *Balneum Mariæ*, which might poſſibly be ſo contrived by the Baſon being large, and capable of working a great many Stills at once, as to be extremely worth the Proprietor's while in all reſpects.

Another Requiſite to be obſerved is, that the Water in the Worm-tub be kept cool ; this may be affected, by placing in the middle of the Tub a wooden Pipe or Gutter, about three Inches ſquare within, reaching from the Top almoſt to the Bottom ; by this Contrivance cold Water may, as often as neceſſary, be conveyed to the Bottom of the Worm-tub, and the hot Water at the Top forced either over the Sides of the Tub, or, which is better, through a leaden Pipe of moderate Size, called a Waſte-pipe, ſoldered into the Top of the Tub, and extended to the Gutter formed to carry away the Water.

CHAP.

C H A P. XVII.

Of the Diftillation of Moloffes Spirits:

THE Spirit diftilled from Moloffes or Treacle, is very clean or pure. It is made from common Treacle diffolved in Water, and fermented in the fame Manner as the Wafh for the common Malt Spirit.

But if fome particular Art is not ufed in Diftilling this Spirit, it will not prove fo vinous as Malt Spirit, but more flat and lefs pungent and acid, though otherwife much cleaner tafted, as its effential Oil is of a lefs offenfive Flavour. Therefore, if good frefh Wine-lees, abounding in Tartar, be added and duly fermented with the Moloffes, the Spirit will acquire a much greater Vinofity and Brifknefs, and approach much nearer to the Nature of foreign Spirits.

Where the Moloffes Spirit is brought to the common Proof Strength, if it be found not to have a fufficient Vinofity, it will be very proper to add fome good dulcified Spirit of Nitre ; and if the Spirit be clean worked, it may, by this Addition only, be made to pafs on ordinary Judges for *French* Brandy.

Great

Great Quantities of this Spirit are used in adulterating foreign Brandy, Rum and Arrac. Much of it is also used alone in making Cherry-Brandy, and other Drams by Infusion ; in all which many, and perhaps with Justice, prefer it to foreign Brandies.

Molosses, like other Spirits, is entirely colourless when first extracted ; but Distillers always give it, as nearly as possible, the Colour of foreign Spirits ; the Methods of performing which we shall explain in a subsequent Chapter.

C H A P. XVIII.

Of the Nature of Brandies, and Method of distilling them in France.

THE general Method of distilling Brandies in *France* need not be formally described, as it differs in nothing from that commonly practised here in working from Wash or Molosses ; nor are they in the least more cleanly, or exact in the Operation.

They only observe more particularly to throw a little of the natural Lee into the Still, along with the Wine, as finding this
gives

gives their Spirit the Flavour, for which it is generally admired abroad.

But though Brandy is extracted from Wine, Experience tells us, that there is a great Difference in Grapes from which the Wine is made. Every Soil, every Climate, every kind of Grapes varies with regard to the Quantity and Quality of Spirits extracted from them. There are fome Grapes which are only fit for eating; others for drying; as thofe of *Damafcus*, *Corinth*, *Provence*, and *Avignon*; but not fit to make Wine.

Some Wines very proper for Diftillation, others much lefs fo. The Wines of *Languedoc* and *Provence* afford a great deal of Brandy by Diftillation, when the Operation is made in their full Strength: The *Orleans* Wines, and thofe of *Blois* afford yet more; but the beft are thofe of the Territories of *Cogniac* and of *Andaye*, which are however in the Number of thofe the leaft drank in *France*. Whereas thofe of *Burgundy* and of *Champaign*, though of a very fine Flavour, are improper, becaufe they yield but very little in Diftillation.

It muft alfo be farther obferved, that all the Wines for Diftillation, as thofe of *Spain*, the *Canaries*, of *Alicant*, of *Cyprus*, of St. *Perés*, of *Toquet*, of *Grave*, of *Hungary*,

and

and others of the fame kind, yield very little Brandy by Diftillation ; and confequently would coft the Diftiller confiderably more than he could fell it for. What is drawn from them is indeed very good, always retaining the faccharine Quality, and rich Flavour of the Wine from whence it is drawn ; but as it grows old, this Flavour often grows aromatic, and is not agreeable to all Palates.

Hence we fee, that Brandies always differ, according as they are extracted from different Species of Grapes. Nor would there be fo great a Similarity as there is between the different kinds of *French* Brandies, were the ftrongeft Wines ufed for this Purpofe : But this is rarely the Cafe, the weakeft and loweft-flavoured Wines only are diftilled for their Spirit, or fuch as prove abfolutely unfit for any other Ufe.

A large Quantity of Brandies is diftilled in *France* during the Time of the Vintage ; for all thofe poor Grapes that prove unfit for Wine, are ufually firft gathered, preffed, their Juice fermented, and directly diftilled. This rids their Hands of their poor Wines at once, and leaves their Cafks empty for the Reception of ·better. It is a general Rule with them not to diftil any Wine, that will fetch any Price as Wine ; for, in this

State,

State, the Profits upon them are vaftly greater than when reduced to Brandies. This large Stock of fmall Wines, with which they are almoft over-run in *France*, fufficiently accounts for their making fuch vaft Quantities of Brandy in *France*, more than other Countries, which lie in warmer Climates, and are much better adapted to the Production of Grapes.

Nor is this the only Fund of their Brandies; for all the Wine that turns eager, is alfo condemned to the Still; and, in fhort, all that they can neither export, nor confume at home, which amounts to a large Quantity; fince much of the Wine, laid in for their Family Provifion, is fo poor, as not to keep during the Time in fpending.

Hence many of our *Englifh* Spirits, with proper Management, are convertable into Brandies, that fhall hardly be diftinguifhed from the foreign in many Refpects, provided this Operation be neatly performed. And, in particular, how far a Cyder Spirit, and a Crab Spirit, may, even from the firft Extraction, be made to refemble the fine and thin Brandies of *France*, we would recommend to thofe Diftillers, whofe Skill and Curiofity prompts them to Undertakings condemned by thofe who only work mechanically, and

fcorn

ſcorn to deviate from the beaten Tract, tho'
they have the faireſt Proſpect of acquiring
Profit to themſelves, and a laſting Emolu-
ment to their Country.

CHAP. XIX.

Of the Diſtillation of Rum.

RUM differs from what we ſimply call
Sugar Spirit, as it contains more of the
natural Flavour, or eſſential Oil of the Sugar Cane ; a great deal of raw Juice, and
even Parts of the Cane itſelf being often
fermented in the Liquor, or Solution, of
which the Rum is prepared.

Hence we ſee from whence Rum derives
its Flavour ; namely, from the Cane itſelf.
Some, indeed, are of Opinion, that the
unctuous or oily Flavour of the Rum proceeds from the large Quantity of Fat uſed
in boiling the Sugar. This Fat, indeed, if
coarſe, will give a ſtinking Flavour to the
Spirit in our Diſtillations of the Sugar Liquor, or Waſh, from our refining Sugar-
houſes ; but this is nothing like the Flavour
of the Rum ; which, as we have already
obſerved, is the Effect of the natural Flavour of the Cane.

Great

Great Quantities of Rum are made at *Jamaica*, *Barbadoes*, *Antigua*, and other Sugar Iflands:. The Method of making it is this :

When a fufficient Stock of the Materials is got together, they add Water to them, and ferment them in the common Method, though the Fermentation is always carried on very flowly at firft ; becaufe at the Beginning of the Seafon for making Rum in the Iflands, they want Yeaft, or fome other Ferment to make it work ; but after this, they, by Degrees, procure a fufficient Quantity of the Ferment, which rifes up as a Head to the Liquor in the Operation ; and thus they are able afterwards to ferment, and make their Rum with a great deal of Expedition, and in very large Quantities.

When the Wafh is fully fermented, or to a due Degree of Acidity, the Diftillation is carried on in the common Way, and the Spirit is made up Proof; though fometimes it is reduced to a much greater Degree of Strength, nearly approaching to that of Alcohol, or Spirit of Wine ; and it is then called double diftilled Rum.

It would be eafy to rectify the Spirit, and bring it to a much greater Degree of Purity

G than.

than we ufually find it to be of ; for it brings
over in the Diftillation a large Quantity of
the Oil ; and this is often fo difagreeable,
that the Rum muft be fuffered to lie by a
long time to mellow before it can be ufed ;
whereas, if well rectified, its Flavour would
be much lefs, and confequently much more
agreeable to the Palate.

The beft State to keep Rum, both for
Exportation, and other Ufes, is doubtlefs
that of Alcohol, or rectified Spirits. In this
manner, it would be contained in half the
Bulk it ufually is, and might be let down
to the common proof Strength with Water
when neceffary : For the common Ufe of
making Punch, it would likewife ferve
much better in the State of Alcohol ; as
the Tafte would be cleaner, and the Strength
might always be regulated to a much greater
Degree of Exactnefs than in the ordinary
Way.

If the Bufinefs of rectifying Rum was
more nicely managed, it feems a very practicable Scheme to throw out fo much of the
Oil, as to reduce it to the fine light State of a
clear Spirit, but lightly impregnated with the
Oil ; in this State it would nearly refemble
Arrac, as is eafily proved by mixing a very
fmall Quantity of it with a taftelefs Spirit ;

for

for it then bears a very near Refemblance to Arrac in Flavour.

CHAP. XX.

Of Sugar-Spirit.

WE mean by a Sugar-Spirit, that extracted from the Wafhings, Scumings, Drofs, and Wafte of a Sugar-baker's Refining-houfe.

Thefe recrementitious, or drofly Parts of the Sugar are to be diluted with Water, fermented in the fame manner as Moloffes or Wafh, and then diftilled in the common Method. And if the Operation be carefully performed, and the Spirit well rectified, it may be mixed with foreign Brandies, and even Arrac in a large Proportion, to great Advantage ; for this Spirit will be found fuperior to that extracted from Treacle, and confequently more proper for thefe Ufes.

CHAP. XXI.

Of Raifin-Spirits.

BY Raifin-Spirits, we underftand, that extracted from Raifins, after a proper Fermentation.

In order to extract this Spirit, the Raifins muſt be infuſed in a proper Quantity of Water, and fermented in the manner deſcribed in the Chapter on Fermentation. When the Fermentation is completed, the whole is to be thrown into the Still, and the Spirit extracted by a ſtrong Fire.

The Reaſon why we here direct a ſtrong Fire, is, becauſe by that Means a greater Quantity of the eſſential Oil will come over the Helm with the Spirit, which will render it much fitter for the Diſtiller's Purpoſe; for this Spirit is generally uſed to mix with common Malt Goods; and it is ſurprizing how far it will go in this Reſpect, ten Gallons of it being often ſufficient to give a determining Flavour, and agreeable Vinoſity to a whole Piece of Malt Spirits.

It is therefore well worth the Diſtiller's while to endeavour at improving the common Method of extracting Spirits from Raifins; and perhaps the following Hint may merit Attention.

When the Fermentation is completed, and the Still charged with fermented Liquor, as above directed, let the whole be drawn off with as briſk a Fire as poſſible; but inſtead of the Caſk or Can, generally
uſed

ufed by our *Englifh* Diftillers for a Receiver,
let a large Glafs, called by Chemifts, a Separating-Glafs, be placed under the Nofe
of the Worm, and a common Receiver
applied to the Spout of the Separating-Glafs;
by this means the effential Oil will fwim
upon the Top of the Spirit, or rather low
Wine, in the Separating-Glafs, and may be
eafily preferved at the End of the Operation.

The Ufe of this limpid effential Oil is well
known to Diftillers; for in this refides the
whole Flavour, and confequently may be
ufed to the greateft Advantage in giving that
diftinguifhing Tafte, and true Vinofity, to
the common Malt-Spirits.

After the Oil is feparated from the low
Wine, the Liquor may be rectified in *Balneum Mariæ* into a pure and almoft taftelefs
Spirit, and therefore well adapted to make
the fineft compound Cordials, or to imitate or mix with the fineft *French* Brandies,
Arracs, *&c.*

In the fame Manner a Spirit may be obtained from Cyder. But as its particular
Flavour is not fo defirable as that obtained
from Raifins, it fhould be diftilled in a more
gentle Manner, and carefully rectified in the
Manner we fhall fhew in the Chapter on

Rectifi-

Rectification; by which Means a very pure and almoſt inſipid Spirit will be obtained, which may be uſed to very great Advantage in imitating the beſt Brandies of *France*, or in making the fineſt compound Waters or Cordials.

CHAP. XXII.

Of Arracs.

WHAT is properly meant by the Term Arracs, are Spirits extracted from the fermented Juice of certain Trees common in the *Eaſt-Indies*, particularly thoſe of the Cocoa, or Palm-tree. The whole Proceſs of making Arrac, is performed in the following Manner.

In order to procure the vegetable Juice for this Operation, the Perſon provides himſelf with a ſufficient Number of ſmall earthen Pots, with Bellies and Necks, reſembling our common glaſs Bottles; a Number of theſe he faſtens to his Girdle, or to a Belt acroſs his Shoulders, and climbs up the tall Trunk of the Cocoa tree: Having reached the Boughs of the Tree, he cuts off with a Knife certain ſmall Buds, or Buttons, applying immediately to the Wound one of his Bottles, and faſtens it with a String to the Bough. In this Manner he

proceeds

proceeds till he has fixed his whole Number of Bottles, which ferve as Receivers
to the Juice diftilling from the Wounds.
This Operation is generally performed in
the Evening, a greater. Quantity of Juice
flowing from the Tree in the Night than in
the Day. The Bottles are next Morning
taken off, and the Liquor emptied with a
proper Veffel, where it fpontaneoufly ferments. As foon as the Fermentation is
completed, the Liquor is thrown into the
Still, and drawn down to a low Wine; but
fo very poor and dilute, that they are obliged to rectify it in another Still, to that
weak kind of Proof Spirit, we generally fee
it; for though it appears Bubble-Proof, it
rarely contains more than a fixth, and fometimes only an eighth of Alcohol, all the
reft being no more than an acidulated Water, which might be fupplied from any common Spring. Why Arrac appears Bubble-
Proof, when in reality fo far below what
we mean by Proof, is not fo great a Myftery,
as at firft Sight it appears to be; for this
kind of Proof is entirely owing to a certain
Tenacity of the Parts of the Liquor, or to
the particular Property of the Oil incorpo-
rated in the Spirit; as we fhall abundantly
fhew in a fubfequent Chapter.

From this Account of Arrac, it fhould
feem no very difficult Matter to imitate it

G 4

here.

here. And, perhaps, the whole Difficulty lies in procuring a pure and infipid Spirit ; for it is ridiculous to attempt it with our common Malt-Spirit. With regard to the Flavour of the Arrac, it may be effectually imitated by fome effential Oils eafily procurable.

Hence we fee of what prodigious Advantage a pure and infipid Spirit would be of to Diftillers, and confequently the great Encouragement there is to attempt the Difcovery. Perhaps a Spirit of this kind may be extracted from Sugar properly refined. The Hint is worth profecuting ; and the Writer of this Effay, from repeated Experiments, is abundantly convinced that the Thing is practicable. Had he entirely fucceeded, he would readily have communicated the Whole for the Benefit of his Country ; but is now obliged to defer, to fome future Opportunity, the Refult of his Enquiries. In the mean Time, he would recommend the Profecution of this Hint to thofe Diftillers, who endeavour to improve their Art, and advance it nearer to Perfection.

Since Arrac is a Spirit extracted from the Juice of the Cocoa tree, it might perhaps be worth enquiring how nearly it might be imitated by fermenting and diftilling the

Juices

Juices of the Birch and Sycamore-trees. We ſhould by this Means obtain an *Engliſh* Arrac; and, perhaps, a Spirit equal in Flavour to that imported from *Batavia*.

When the Caſk, in which the Arrac is imported happens to be decayed; or the Liquor touches any Nails, or other Iron, it diſſolves Part of it, and at the ſame time extracts the reſinous Parts of the Oak, by which means the whole Liquor in the Caſk acquires an inky Colour. In order to whiten and clarify Arrac, which has contracted this Colour, a large Quantity of new or ſkimed Milk muſt be put into the Caſk, and the whole beat together, as Vintners do to whiten their brown Wines; by this means the inky Colour will be abſorbed by the Milk, and fall with it to the Bottom, ſo that the greateſt Part of the Arrac may be drawn off fine; and the Remainder procured in the ſame Condition by being filtrated through a conical Flannel Bag.

CHAP. XXIII.

Of Rectification.

THERE are ſeveral Methods of performing this Operation; though ſome, and indeed thoſe in general practiſed by our Diſtillers, hardly deſerve the Name; becauſe inſtead inftead of rectifying,.that is freeing the Spirit from its effential Oil and Phlegm, they alter the natural Flavour of the Spirit·that comes over in the Operation.

The principal Bufinefs of Rectification is to feparate the Spirit from the effential Oil of the Ingredient, which is very apt to.adhere ftrongly to the Spirit. And in order to this, Care fhould be.taken in the firft Diftillation ; that is, the Spirit, efpecially that from Malt, fhould be drawn by a gentle Fire. by which means great Part of the effential Oil will be kept from mixing with the Spirit ; for Experience has abundantly proved, that it is much eafier to keep afunder, than to feparate them when once mixed.

But as it is almoft impoffible to draw low Wines without the Spirit being in fome Meafure impregnated with the effential Oil, it is abfolutely neceffary to be acquainted with. fome Methods of feparating the Spirit from the Oil, and alfo of freeing it from its Phlegm. The beft Methods of doing this to Perfection, are Re-diftillation and Percolation.

In order to rectify low Wines, they fhould be put into a tall Body or Alembic, and gently diftilled in *Balneum Mariæ* ; by this
means

means a large Proportion, both of the Oil and Phlegm will remain in the Body. But if the Spirit fhould be found, after this Operation, to contain fome of the effential Oil, it muft be let down with fair Water, and re-diftilled in the fame gentle Manner. And thus it may be brought to any Degree of Purity; efpecially if in the working the Spirit be fuffered to fall into a proper Quantity of clear Water, and the Spirit afterwards rectified to the Height propofed. The fame Method fhould be ufed in freeing Proof-Spirit, or even Alcohol, from this Oil; namely, by letting it down with clean Water to the Strength of low Wines, and re-diftilling it in *Balneum Mariæ*. But it muft be remembered, that it is much more difficult to cleanfe Alcohol, or Proof-Spirit than low Wines, becaufe the Oil is more intimately mixed with the two former than with the latter. This Oil may however be feparated from Proof-Spirit, &c. by the Method already propofed, efpecially if it be previoufly filtrated through Paper, thick Flannel, Sand, Stone, &c.

But this Method, though it effectually anfwers the Intention, is generally rejected by our Diftillers, becaufe of the Slownefs of the Operation ; and others fubftituted in its ftead, though inftead of freeing the Spirit from the Oil, they only abolifh the natural

Flavour

Flavour of the Spirit, and make a more intimate Mixture between the Particles of the Spirit, and thofe of the effential Oil.

It is impoffible to enumerate all the Methods practifed by Diftillers, as almoft every one pretends to have a fecret Noftrum for this Purpofe. The principal Methods in ufe for rectifying Malt-Spirits, are however reducible to three, namely, by fixed alcaline Salts, by acid Spirits mixed with alcaline Salts, and by faline Bodies, and flavouring Additions.

The Method of rectifying by alcaline Salts is thus performed. To every Piece of Proof-Spirit, add fourteen Pounds of dry Salt of Tartar, fixed Nitre, or calcined Tartar; lute on the Head, and diftil, by a gentle Heat, but be very careful to leave out the Faints. By this Method a large Proportion of the fœtid Oil will be left in the Still; and what comes over with the Spirit will be greatly attenuated. But this Operation is generally performed in a very different manner; for, inftead of diftilling the the Spirit in a gentle and equable manner, the Still is worked in its full Force; by which means the Oil, which fhould have remained in the Still, is driven over, and intimately mixed with the Spirit; and, confequently, the whole Operation fruftrated,

and

and the Spirit rendered much harder to cleanfe than it was before.

But even when the Operation is performed according to the Rules of Art, it is far from being perfect; for it is well known, that Part of the fixed Salts become volatile in the Operation, pafs over the Helm, and intimately mixes with the effential Oil ftill contained in the Spirits: by this means the Oil becomes more perfectly united with the Spirits, and confequently much harder to be feparated by repeated Diftillations. Nor is this all, for the Still being worked in its full Force, the bitter Oil of the Malt, formed into a kind of liquid Soap in the Still, by means of the alcaline Salt, is brought over the Helm with the Faints, and fuffered to mix with the Spirit, whereby it is rendered almoft as naufeous and illtafted as before the Operation. Befides, if this Operation were performed in its utmoft Perfection, it would never anfwer the Intention; for the alcaline Salt deftroys the Vinofity of the Spirit; and confequently deprives it of one of its moft valuable Properties. Our Diftillers are well acquainted with this Defect in the Operation, and endeavour to fupply it by an Addition of Acids. This is what we call the fecond Method by Alcalies and Acids.

The

The Operation of rectifying by the Method of fixed Alcalies and Acids is the ſame as that above deſcribed ; the Spirit is drawn over from fixed Alcalies as before ; but in order to mortify the Alcali in the Spirit, and reſtore its Vinoſity, a proper Quantity of ſome acid Spirit is added. Various kinds of Acids are uſed on this Occaſion ; but principally thoſe of the mineral Kind, becauſe of their Cheapneſs ; as Oil of Vitriol, Spirit of Nitre, Oil of Sulphur, and the like. We would, however, caution a young Diſtiller from being too buſy with theſe corroſive Acids, the ſulphurous Spirit of Vitriol, dulcified Spirit of Nitre, or Mr. *Boyle*'s acid Spirit of Wine well rectified, will much better anſwer his Purpoſe.

The third Method of Rectification is that by ſaline Bodies, and flavouring Ingredients. There is no Difference in the Operation between this and the two foregoing Methods ; fixed alcaline Salts, common Salt decrepitated or dried, calcined Vitriol, Sandiver, Allum, &c. is put into the Still with the low Wines, and the Spirit drawn over as before. When the Quantity is drawn off, the flavouring Ingredients are added to give the Spirit the Flavour intended. But as the Spirit is not by this means rendered ſufficiently pure, the diſagreeable Flavour of

the

the Spirit generally overpowers that of the Ingredients, whereby the whole Intention is either deftroyed, or a compound Flavour produced, very different from that intended.

Some Diftillers, inftead of alcaline Salts, ufe quick Lime in rectifying their Malt Spirit; this Ingredient cleanfes and dephlegmates the Spirit confiderably; but like that rectified from alcaline Salts, it requires an alcaline Difpofition, and alfo an nidorous Flavour. Acids, therefore, are as neceffary to be mixed with thofe Spirits rectified with quick Lime, as with thofe rectified with an alcaline Salt. If Chalk, calcined and well purified animal Bones, &c. were ufed inftead of quick Lime, the Spirit would have a much lefs alcaline or nidorous Flavour; and, confequently, the flavouring Ingredients might be added to it with more Succefs than can be expected from a Spirit rectified from alcaline Salts.

But, perhaps, if neutral Salts were ufed inftead of the alcaline ones, the Spirit might be rendered pure, without contracting an alcaline Flavour; foluble Tartar might be ufed for this Purpofe, though the Spirit acquires from hence a little faponaceous Flavour. Dr. *Cox* has mentioned another Method

thod for this Purpofe, namely, to deprive the volatile Salts of their Oil, by rendering them neutral with Spirit of Salt, and afterwards fubliming them with Salt of Tartar: The Acid may be varied if the Spirit of Salt fhould not be found fo well adapted to the Purpofe as could be wifhed: But fine dry Sugar feems the beft adapted to the Purpofe of rectifying thefe Spirits; as it readily unites with the effential Oil, detains and fixes it, without imparting any urinous, alcaline, or other naufeous Flavour to the Spirits rectified upon it.

Thus have I confidered the principal Methods ufed by our Diftillers in rectifying their Spirits; and fhall conclude this Chapter with remarking, that there is no other Way of rectifying to Perfection befides what we firft laid down, namely, by gentle Diftillation. But then it muft be remembered, that the whole Procefs muft be of a Piece: We mean, that the firft Diftillation from the Wafh muft be performed in a gentle manner; for otherwife the effential Oil will be fo intimately blended with the Spirit, as not to be eafily feparated by Re-diftillation. Another good Property attending this Method is its Univerfality; all kinds of Spirits, from whatever Ingredients extracted, require Rectification; and this is adapted to all kinds.

C H A P.

CHAP. XXIV.

Of the Flavouring of Spirits.

WE have obferved in the preceding Chapter, that the common Method of rectifying Spirits from alcaline Salts, deftroys their Vinofity, and in its ftead introduces an urinous or lixivious Tafte. But as it is abfolutely neceffary to reftore, or at leaft to fubftitute in its room fome Degree of Vinofity, feveral Methods have been propbfed, and a Multitude of Experiments performed, in order to difcover this great *Defideratum :* But none has fucceeded equal to the Spirit of Nitre ; and accordingly this Spirit, either ftrong or dulcified, has been ufed by moft Diftillers to give an agreeable Vinofity to their Spirits.

Several Difficulties however occur in the Method of ufing it ; the principal of which is, its being apt to quit the Liquor in a fhort Time, and confequently depriving the Liquor of that Vinofity it was intended to give. In order to remove this Difficulty, and prevent the Vinofity from quitting the Goods, the dulcified Spirit of Nitre, which is much better than the ftrong Spirit, fhould be prepared by a previous Digeftion continued for fome Time with Alcohol ; the

H longer

perhaps a preparation of Æther — woud answer that end beft.

longer the Digeſtion is continued the more intimately will they be blended, and the Compound rendered the milder and ſofter.

After a proper Digeſtion, the dulcified Spirit ſhould be mixed with the Brandy, by which Means the Vinoſity will be intimately blended with the Goods, and diſpoſed not to fly off for a very conſiderable Time.

No general Rule can be given for the Quantity of this mineral Acid requiſite to be employed, becauſe different Proportions of it are neceſſary in different Spirits. It ſhould, however, be carefully adverted to, that though a ſmall Quantity of it will undoubtedly give an agreeable Vinoſity reſembling that naturally found in the fine ſubtile Spirits drawn from Wines, yet an over large Doſe of it will not only cauſe a diſagreeable Flavour, but alſo render the whole Deſign abortive, by diſcovering the Impoſition. Thoſe, therefore, who endeavour to cover a foul Taſte in Goods by large Doſes of dulcified Spirit of Nitre, will find themſelves deceived.

But the beſt, and indeed the only Method of imitating *French* Brandies to Perfection, is by an eſſential Oil of Wine; this being the very thing that gives the *French* Brandies their Flavour. It muſt, however,

however, be remembered, that in order to uſe even this Ingredient to Advantage, a pure, taſteleſs Spirit muſt be firſt procured ; for it is ridiculous to expect that this eſſential Oil ſhould be able to give the agreeable Flavour of *French* Brandies, to our fulſome Malt Spirit, already loaded with its own nauſeous Oil, or ſtrongly impregnated with a lixivious Taſte from the alcaline Salts uſed in Rectification. How a pure inſipid Spirit may be obtained has been already conſidered in ſome of the preceding Chapters ; it only therefore remains to ſhew the Method of procuring this eſſential Oil of Wine, which is this :

Take ſome Cakes of dry Wine Lees, ſuch as are uſed by our Hatters, diſſolve them in ſix or eight times their Weight of Water, diſtil the Liquor with a ſlow Fire, and ſeparate the Oil by the Separating Glaſs ; reſerving for the niceſt Uſes that only which comes over firſt, the ſucceeding Oil being coarſer and more reſinous.

Having procured this fine Oil of Wine, it may be mixed into a Quinteſſence with pure Alcohol ; by which Means it may be preſerved a long time fully poſſeſſed of all its Flavour and Virtues ; but without ſuch Management, it will ſoon grow reſinous and rancid.

H 2 When

When a fine essential Oil of Wine is thus procured, and also a pure and insipid Spirit, *French* Brandies may be imitated to Perfection with regard to the Flavour. It must, however, be remembered, and carefully adverted to, that the essential Oil be drawn from the same sort of Lees, as the Brandy to be imitated was procured from; we mean, in order to imitate *Coniac* Brandy, it will be necessary to distil the essential Oil from *Coniac* Lees; and the same for any other kind of Brandy. For as different Brandies have different Flavours; and as these Flavours are owing entirely to the essential Oil of the Grape, it would be preposterous to endeavour to imitate the Flavour of *Coniac* Brandy, with an essential Oil procured from the Lees of *Bourdeaux* Wine.

When the Flavour of the Brandy is well imitated by a proper Dose of the essential Oil, and the Whole reduced into one simple and homogeneous Fluid, other Difficulties are still behind : The Flavour, though the essential Part, is not however the only one; the Colour, the Proof and the Softness must be also regarded, before a Spirit, that perfectly resembles Brandy, can be procured. With regard to the Proof, it may be easily hit, by using a Spirit rectified

tified above Proof ; which, after being intimately mixed with the eſſential Oil of Wine, may be let down to a proper Standard by fair Water. And the Softneſs may in a great Meaſure be obtained by diſtilling and rectifying the Spirit with a gentle Fire; and what is wanting of this Criterion in the Liquor, when firſt made, will be ſupplied by Time ; for it muſt be remembered, that it is Time alone that gives this Property to *French* Brandies ; they being at firſt, like our Spirits, acrid, foul, and fiery. But with regard to the Colour a particular Method is neceſſary to imitate it to Perfection : And how this may be done ſhall be conſidered in the next Chapter.

C H A P. XXV.

Of the Methods of colouring Spirits.

THE Art of colouring Spirits owes its Riſe to Obſervations on foreign Brandies. A Piece of *French* Brandy that has acquired by Age a great Degree of Softneſs and Ripeneſs is obſerved, at the ſame time, to have acquired a yellowiſh brown Colour ; and hence our Diſtillers have endeavoured to imitate this Colour in ſuch Spirits as are intended to paſs for *French* Brandy. And in order to this a great Variety of Experiments has been made on various Subſtances,

H 3　　　　in

in order to difcover a direct and fure Method of imitating this Colour to Perfection. But, in order to do this, it is neceffary to know from whence the *French* Brandies themfelves acquire their Colour ; for till we have made this Difcovery, it will be in vain to attempt an Imitation ; becaufe, if we fhould be able to imitate exactly the Colour, which is indeed no difficult Tafk, the Spirit will not ftand the Teft of different Experiments, unlefs the Colour in both be produced from the fame Ingredient.

This being undeniably the Cafe, let us try if we cannot difcover this mighty Secret; the Ingredient from whence the *French* Brandy acquires its Colour.

We have already obferved, that this Colour is only found in fuch Brandies as have acquired a mellow Ripenefs by Age ; it is therefore not given it by the Diftiller, but has gained it by lying long in the Cafk. Confequently, the Ingredient from whence this Colour is extracted, is no other than the Wood of the Cafk, and the Brandy in reality is become a dilute Tincture of Oak.

The common Experiment ufed to prove the Genuinenefs of *French* Brandy proves, that this Opinion is well founded. The Ex-

Experiment is this : They pour into a Glaſs of Brandy a few Drops of a Solution of calcined Vitriol of Iron in a diluted Spirit of Sulphur, or any other mineral Acid, and the Whole turns of a blue Colour ; in the ſame Manner, as we make Ink of a Tincture of Galls and Vitriol.

Since, therefore, the Colour of *French* Brandies is acquired from the Oak of the Caſk, it is no Difficulty to imitate it to Perfection. A ſmall Quantity of the Extract of Oak, or the Shavings of that Wood properly digeſted, will furniſh us with a Tincture capable of giving the Spirit any Degree of Colour required. But it muſt be remembered, that as the Tincture is extracted from the Caſk by Brandy, that is Alcohol and Water, it is neceſſary to uſe both in extracting the Tincture ; for each of theſe Menſtruums diſſolves different Parts of the Wood. Let, therefore, a ſufficient Quantity of Oak Shavings be digeſted in ſtrong Spirit of Wine ; and alſo at the ſame Time other Oak Shavings be digeſted in Water : And when the Liquors have acquired a ſtrong Tincture from the Oak, let both be poured off from the Shavings, into different Veſſels, and both placed over a gentle Fire till reduced to the Conſiſtence of Treacle. In this Condition, let the two

H 4 Ex-

Extracts be intimately mixed together; which may be done effectually by adding a small Quantity of Loaf Sugar, in fine Powder, and well rubbing the Whole together. By this Means a liquid essential Extract of Oak will be procured, and always ready to be used as Occasion shall require.

There are other Methods in Use for colouring Brandies; but the best, besides the Extract of Oak above-mentioned, are common Treacle and burnt Sugar.

The Treacle gives the Spirits a fine Colour, nearly resembling that of *French* Brandy; but as its Colour is but dilute, a large Quantity must be used; this is not however attended with any bad Consequences; for notwithstanding the Spirit is really weakened by this Addition, yet the bubble Proof, the general Criterion of Spirits, is greatly mended by the Tenacity imparted to the Liquor by the Treacle. The Spirit also acquires from this Mixture a sweetish or luscious Taste, and a Fulness in the Mouth; both which Properties render it very agreeable to the Palates of the common People, who are, in fact, the principle Consumers of these Spirits.

A

A much fmaller Quantity of burnt Sugar than of Treacle will be fufficient for colouring the fame Quantity of Spirits; the Tafte is alfo very different; for, inftead of the Sweetnefs imparted by the Treacle, the Spirit acquires from the burnt Sugar an agreeable Bitternefs, and by that Means recommends itfelf to nicer Palates, which are offended with a lufcious Spirit. The burnt Sugar is prepared by diffolving a proper Quantity of Sugar in a little Water, and fcorching it over the Fire till it acquires a black Colour.

Either of the above Ingredients, Treacle or burnt Sugar, will nearly imitate the genuine Colour of old *French* Brandy; but neither of them will fucceed, when put to the Teft of the vitriolic Solution.

Thus have I traced the Subject of Diftillation from its Origin; fhewn the Methods commonly made ufe of by Diftillers, and pointed out various Improvements, that might be introduced into this Art with great Advantage; and fhall conclude this Part with recommending the feveral Hints to thofe Diftillers who are defirous of improving their Art, and proceeding on a rational Foundation, it being from fuch only

that

that Improvements are to be expected; for where the Operations are constantly carried on in the same beaten Tract, it is in vain to expect Improvements, unless Chance should be kind enough to throw that in their Way, which a rational Theory would have easily led them to discover.

A

A

Complete System

OF

DISTILLATION.

PART II.

Containing the Method of distilling Simple Waters.

CHAP. I.

THE Instruments chiefly used in the Distillation of Simple Waters, are of two Kinds, commonly called the *Hot Still*, or Alembic, and the *Cold Still*; the former is represented in *Fig. 5.* and the latter in *Fig. 10.*

The

The Waters drawn by the cold Still from odoriferous Plants are much more fragrant, and more fully impregnated with their Virtues than those drawn by the hot Still, or Alembic; but the Operation is much more slow and tedious by the former than the latter, so that very few care to comply with it: And, therefore a Method has been invented, to avoid the Tediousness of the one, and the Inconveniencies of the other. The Method is this:

A Pewter Body is suspended in the Body of the Alembic, and the Head of the Still fitted to the Pewter Body: Into this Body the Ingredients to be distilled are put, the Alembic filled with Water, the Still Head luted to the Pewter Body, and the Nose luted into the Worm of the Refrigeratory or Worm.

The same Intention will be answered, by putting the Ingredients into a Glass Alembic, and placing it in a Bath Heat, or *Balneum Mariæ*; as we have before directed, Chap. XI.

By either of these Means, the Ingredients have greater Heat given them than in the cold Still; and yet, by the Interposition of the Water, in which the Vessel,

containing

containing them is placed, they are not fo
forcibly acted upon by the Fire, as in the
common Way of the hot Still. So that all
thofe Things which require a middle Way
between the other; that is, thofe Simples
which are of a Texture between very volatile, and very fixed, are treated very properly by this Method; but neither the very
odoriferous Simples, nor thofe whofe Parts
are very heavy and fixed, can be treated this
Way but to Difadvantage.

One of the greateft Advantages of this
Contrivance is, that Waters fo drawn come
over much cooler than from the hot Still;
that is, they have not fo much of the Fire
in them, as the Diftillers term it; fo that
a hot fpicy Water, thus ordered, will tafte
as cool on the Palate when juft drawn, as it
would, when drawn by the hot Still, after
it had acquired a confiderable Age.

CHAP. II.

Of Waters drawn by the cold Still.

THE cold Still is much beft adapted
to draw off the Virtues of Simples,
which are valued for their fine Flavour
when green, which is fubject to be loft in
drying. For when we want to extract from
Plants a Spirit fo light and volatile, as not

to subsist in open Air any longer than while the Plant continues in its Growth, it is certainly the best Method to remove the Plant from its native Soil, into some proper Instrument, where, as it dries, these volatile Parts can be collected and preserved. And such an Instrument is what we call the cold Still, where the drying of the Plant or Flower, is only forwarded by a moderate Warmth, and all that rises is collected and preserved.

As the Method of performing the Operation by the cold Still, is the very same, whatever Plant or Flower is used, the following Instance of procuring a Water from Rosemary, will be abundantly sufficient to instruct the young Practitioner in the manner of conducting the Process in all Cases whatever.

Take Rosemary, fresh gathered, in its Perfection, with the Morning Dew upon it, and lay it lightly and unbruised upon the Plate, or Bottom of the Still. Cover the Plate with its conical Head, and apply a Glass Receiver to the Nose of it. Make a small Fire of Charcoal under the Plate, continuing it as long as any Liquor comes over into the Receiver. When nothing more comes over, take off the Still Head, and remove the Plant, putting fresh in its stead, ftead, and proceed as before; continue to repeat the Operation fucceffively, till a fufficient Quantity of Water is procured. Let this diftilled Water be kept at Reft, in clean Bottles clofe ftopped, for fome Days in a cold Place; by this Means it will become limpid, and powerfully impregnated with the Tafte and Smell of the Plant.

In this Water are contained the Liquor of Dew, confifting of its own proper Parts, which are not without Difficulty feparated from the Plant, and cleave to it even in the drying. This Dew, alfo, by fticking to the Outfide, receives the liquid Parts of the Plant, which being elaborated the Day before, and exhaling in the Night, are hereby detained; fo that they concrete together into one external Liquid, which is often vifcid, as appears in Manna, Honey, &c. This Water alfo contains the Fluid, which exhales from the Veffels of the Rofemary, and which principally confifts of fimple Water, as appears upon long ftanding in an open Veffel, when the Tafte and Odour vanifhing, leave an infipid Water behind. Another Part of this Water is that fubtile, volatile Subftance, which give the Plant its peculiar Tafte and Odour; for this the Senfes difcover in it; but what remains after the Procefs is finifhed, fcarce afford any thing thereof. The fame Water feems

alfo

also to contain Seeds, or other little Bodies, which in a certain Time usually grows into a kind of thin, whitish Weed, suspended in the middle of the Water; and daily increasing or spreading itself, becomes a Mucilage, which did not appear at first.

I have kept these Waters undisturbed in separate well closed Vessels, and observed that in a Year's Time, they began to appear thick, which Thickness gradually increased every Year, till at length the Liquor grew ropy and mucilaginous. Hence we see, that this Water contains the elementary Water, and presiding Spirit of the Plant; a Spirit small in Bulk, but rich in Virtues, and exhibiting the specific Smell and Taste of the Subject. This Water, therefore, in exhaling, proves a Vehicle to that Spirit, which contains in a small, subtile, extremely volatile, and thence easily separable Substance; the particular Virtue of the Plant, leaving the Remainder exhausted in this Respect: and hence proceeds the medicinal Virtues of these Waters, which principally depend upon their native Spirit. For this Spirit, in most Plants, having a brisk Mobility, affects the Nerves, and raises the Spirits in case of their Depression.

If the Vessel be close stopped, and set in a cool Place, the Waters drawn by the cold

Still

ſtill will retain their Virtues for a Year; but if negligently kept, or any Crack ſhould happen in the Glaſs, their extremely volatile Spirit ſecretly flies off, and leaves the Water vapid.

Hence we learn what it is that Plants loſe by being dried in the Summer-time; namely, the Water and Spirit we have been deſcribing. Hence we alſo know the Nature of that Fluid, which firſt riſes from Plants in Diſtillation, and what that Matter properly is in Plants, that gives their peculiar Odour; that is, their preſiding Spirit. Laſtly, we hence learn, in ſome meaſure at leaſt, what thoſe *Effluvia* are, which principally in the Summer-Seaſon, and in the open Air, exhale from Vegetables; for it is highly probable, that theſe conſtant Exhalations of Plants, eſpecially in the Day-time, have a near Agreement in their peculiar Nature, with the Liquor extracted by the cold Still, though differing in this, that the Exhalation made from the Parts is continually recruited by the Root; whilſt by our Operation, thoſe Parts alone are collected, which are driven off from the Plant, after being gathered, and no longer ſupplied with freſh Nouriſhment.

I CHAP.

CHAP. II.

Of the Diſtilling Simple Waters by the Alembic.

THE Plants deſigned for this Operation are to be gathered when their
Leaves are at full Growth, and a little before
the Flowers appear, or, at leaſt, before
the Seed comes on ; becauſe the Virtue of
the Simple expected in theſe Waters is often
little, after the Seed or Fruit is formed,
at which Time Plants begin to languiſh :
The Morning is beſt to gather them in,
becauſe the volatile Parts are then con-
denſed by the Coldneſs of the Night, and
kept in by the Tenacity of the Dew, not
yet exhaled by the Sun.

This is to be underſtood, when the Virtue of the diſtilled Water reſides principally
in the Leaves of Plants ; as it does in Mint,
Marjoram, Pennyroyal, Rue, and many
more ; but the Caſe differs when the aromatic Virtue is only found in the Flowers,
as in Roſes, Lillies of the Valley, &c. in
which Caſe we chooſe their flowery Parts,
whilſt they ſmell the ſweeteſt, and gather
them before they are quite opened, or begin to ſhed, the morning Dew ſtill hanging on them.

In

In other Plants the Seeds are to be preferred, as in Aniſe, Caraway, Cumin, &c. where
the Herb and the Flower are indolent, and
the whole reſides in the Seed alone, where it
manifeſts itſelf by its remarkable Fragrance,
and aromatic Taſte. We find that Seeds
are more fully poſſeſſed of this Virtue, when
they arrive at perfect Maturity.

We muſt not omit that theſe deſirable
Properties are found only in the Roots of
certain Plants, as appears in Avens and in
Orpine, whoſe Roots ſmell like a Roſe.
Roots of this Kind ſhould be gathered, for
the preſent Purpoſe, at that Time when
they are richeſt in theſe Virtues; which is
generally at that Seaſon of the Year, juſt
before they begin to ſprout, when they are
to be dug up in a Morning.

If the Virtues here required be contained in the Barks or Woods of Vegetables, then theſe Parts muſt be choſen for
the Purpoſe.

The Subject being choſen, let it be bruiſed,
or cut, if there be occaſion, and with it
fill two thirds of a Still, leaving a third
Part of it empty, without ſqueezing the
Matter cloſe; then pour as much Rain or
River Water into the Still as will fill it to

I 2   the

the same Height; that is, two thirds together with the Plant: Fit on the Head, luting the Juncture, so that no Vapour may pass through; and also lute the Nose of the Still-head to the Worm. Apply a Receiver to the Bottom of the Worm, that no Vapour may fly off in the Distillation; but that all the Vapour being condensed in the Worm, by cold Water in the Worm-tub, may be collected in the Receiver.

Let the Plant remain thus in the Still to digest for twenty-four Hours, with a small Degree of Heat. Afterwards raise the Fire, so as to make the Water in the Still boil; which may be known by a certain hissing Noise, proceeding from the breaking Bubbles of the boiling Matter; as also by the Pipe of the Still-head, or the upper-end of the Worm, becoming too hot to be handled; or the smoaking of the Water in the Worm-tub heated by the Top of the Worm; and, lastly, by the following of one Drop immediately after another, from the Nose of the Worm, so as to form an almost continual Stream. By all these Signs we know that the requisite Heat is given; if it be less than a gentle Ebullition, the Virtues of the Simple, here expected, will not be raised: On the contrary, when the Fire is too strong, the Water hastily rises into the Still-head, and fouls both the Worm and the

the diſtilled Liquor ; and the Plant being alſo raiſed, it blocks up the Worm ; for which Reaſon it is no bad Caution to faſten a-piece of fine Linen before the Pipe of the Still-head ; that, in caſe of this Accident, the Plant may be kept from ſtopping up the Worm : But, notwithſtanding this Precaution, if the Fire be too fierce, the Plant will ſtop up the Pipe of the Still-head ; and, conſequently, the riſing Vapour finding no Paſſage, will blow off the Still-head, and throw the boiling Liquor about the Still-houſe, ſo as to do a great deal of Miſchief, and even ſuffocate the Operator, without a proper Caution ; and the more oily, tenacious, gummy, or reſinous the Subject is, the greater the Danger, in caſe of this Accident ; becauſe the Liquor is the more frothy and exploſive.

Let the due Degree of Fire therefore be carefully obſerved, and equally kept up, as long as the Water, diſtilling into the Receiver, is white, thick, odorous, ſapid, frothy and turbid ; for this Water muſt be carefully kept ſeparate from that which follows it. The Receiver, therefore, ſhould be often changed, that the Operator may be certain that nothing but this firſt Water comes over ; for there afterwards ariſes a Water that is tranſparent, thin, and without the peculiar Taſte and Flavour of the

I 3   Plant,

Plant, but generally ſomewhat tartariſh and limpid, though ſomewhat obſcured and fouled by white dreggy Matter : And if the Head of the Still be of Copper, and not tinned, the Acidity of this laſt Water corrodes the Copper, ſo as to become green, nauſeous, emetic and poiſonous to thoſe who uſe it, eſpecially to Children, and Perſons of weak Conſtitutions.

The firſt Water above-deſcribed, principally contains the Oil and preſiding Spirit of the Plant ; for the Fire by boiling the Subject, diſſolves its Oil, and reduces it into ſmall Particles, which are carried upwards by the Aſſiſtance of the Water, along with thoſe Parts of the Plant that become volatile with their Motion. And, if the Veſſels are exactly cloſed, all theſe being united together, will be diſcharged without Loſs, and without much Alteration, into the Receiver ; and, conſequently, furniſh us with a Water richly impregnated with the Smell, Taſte, and particular Virtues of the volatile Parts of the Plants it was extracted from.

The Water of the ſecond Running, wants the volatile Part above deſcribed, and has ſcarce any other Virtue than that of cooling.

And

And this is the beft Method of preparing fimple Waters, provided the two forts be not mixed together, for both of them would be fpoiled by fuch a Mixture.

Hence it plainly appears at what time, with the fame Degree of Fire, quite contrary Virtues may arife from a Plant; for fo long as a milk Water continues to come over from fuch Plants as are aromatic, fo long the Water remains warming and attenuating; but when it comes to be thin and pellucid, it is acid and cooling.

Hence we may alfo learn the true Foundation for conducting of Diftillation; for if the Operation be ftopped, as foon as ever the white Water ceafes to come over, the Preparation will be valuable and perfect; but if, through a Defire of increafing that Quantity, more be drawn off, and the latter acid Part fuffered to mix with the firft Running, the whole will be fpoiled, or at leaft rendered greatly inferior to what it would otherwife have been.

Such is the general Method of procuring fimple Waters, that fhall contain the volatile Virtues of the Plants diftilled; fome Rules are however neceffary to render it

I 4   appli-

applicable to all Sorts of Plants; thefe Rules are the following:

1. Let the aromatic, balfamic, oily, and ftrong-fmelling Plants, which long retain their natural Fragrance, fuch as Balm, Hyffop, Juniper, Marjoram, Mint, Origanum, Pennyroyal, Rofemary, Lavender, Sage, &c. be gently dried a little in the Shade; then digeft them, in the fame manner as already mentioned, for twenty-four Hours, in a clofe Veffel, with a fmall Degree of Heat, and afterwards diftil in the manner above delivered, and thus they will afford excellent Waters.

2. When Waters are to be' drawn from Barks, Roots, Seeds, or Woods that are very denfe, ponderous, tough and refinous, let them be digefted for three, four, or more Weeks, with a greater Degree of Heat, in a clofe Veffel, with a proper Quantity of Salt added, to open and prepare them the better for Diftillation. The Quantity of Sea-falt is here added, partly to open the Subject the more, but chiefly to prevent Putrefaction, which otherwife would certainly happen in fo long a Time, and with fuch a Heat as is neceffary in this Cafe, and fo deftroy the Smell, Tafte, and Virtues expected from the Procefs.

3.

3. Thofe Plants which diffufe their Odour to fome Diftance from them, and thus foon lofe it, fhould immediately be diftilled after being gathered in a proper Seafon, without any previous Digeftion; thus Borage, Buglofs, Jeffamin, white Lilies, Lilies of the Valley, Rofes, &c. are hurt by Heat, Digeftion, or lying in the Air.

C H A P. III.

Of increafing the Virtues of Simple Waters by means of Cohobation.

BY Cohobation is meant the returning the diftilled Water procured in the manner defcribed in the preceding Chapter, upon more of the frefh Plant. The Operation is performed in the following manner:

Take the Plant and Liquor remaining in the Still after the Operation defcribed in the foregoing Chapter is performed, and prefs them ftrongly in a Bag for that Purpofe, that all the Decoction may be obtained; and with this mix all the Water before drawn over. Return this Mixture into the Still, and a frefh Quantity of the fame Plant, and if neceffary, as much Water as will make the former Proportion to

the

the Plant. Clofe all the Junctures exactly, and digeft the whole in a gentle Degree of Heat for three Days and three Nights, that the Herb, being fo long fteeped in its own Liquor, may be opened, loofened, and difpofed the eafier to part with its Virtues. This Digeftion is of great Service; but if protracted too long, introduces a Change tending to Putrefaction. Let the Water now be diftilled off, in the fame manner as before; only proceeding more cautioufly, and fomewhat more flowly at firft; becaufe the Liquor in the Still being now thicker, more impregnated with the Plant, and therefore more apt to fmell upon feeling the Fire, it eafily boils over; but after about half of the expected Water is come off, the Fire may be gradually raifed.

By this Method, and carefully obferving to change the Receiver, as foon as the firft Water is all come over, a noble Liquor, highly impregnated with the Virtues of the Plant, will be obtained. And as this Operation may be repeated as often as defired, the Virtues of Plants may be thus exalted to any Degree the Artift fhall think proper; which fhews the extraordinary Power of Diftillation. This Method I would particularly recommend for making the fimple Water of Balm, Elder Flowers, Rofes, and

and the like Simples, but fparingly furnifhed with an effential Oil.

CHAP. IV.

Of the Method of procuring a fimple Water from Vegetables, by previoufly fermenting the Vegetable before Diftillation.

BY this elegant Method we obtain the Virtues of Plants very little altered from what they naturally are, though rendered much more penetrating and volatile. The Operation is performed in the following manner.

Take a fufficient Quantity of any recent Plant, cut it, and bruife it if neceffary; put it into a Cafk, leaving a Space empty at top of about four Inches deep; then take as much Water as would, when added, fill the Cafk to the fame Height, including the Plant, and mix therein about an eighth Part of Honey, if it be cold Winter Weather; or a twelfth Part, if it be warm : In the Summer the like Quantity of coarfe, unrefined Sugar might be added inftead of Honey, or half an Ounce of Yeaft to each Pint of Water will have the fame Effect; though moft prefer Honey for this Purpofe. When the proper Quantity of Honey is added to the Water, let it be warmed and
poured

poured into the Cask, and set it in a warm Place to ferment for two or three Days; but the Herb must not be suffered to fall to the Bottom, nor the Fermentation above half finished. The Whole must then be immediately committed to the Still, and the Fire raised by Degrees; for the Liquor, containing much fermenting Spirit, easily rarefies with the Fire, froths, swells, and therefore becomes very subject to boil over; we ought therefore to work slower, especially at first.

By this Method there will come over at first, a limpid, unctuous, penetrating, odorous, sapid Liquor, which is to be kept separate: After this there follows a milky, opake, turbid Liquor, still containing something of the same Taste and Odour; and at length comes one that is thin, acid, without either Smell, or scarce any Property of the Plant.

The first Water, or rather Spirit, may be kept several Years, in a close Vessel, without changing or growing ropy. It also excellently retains the Taste and Odour of the Plant, though a little altered; but if less Honey were added, less Heat employed, or the Fermentation continued for a smaller Time, the distilled Liquor of the

first

firft running would be white, thick, opake, unctuous, frothy, and perfectly retain the Scent and Tafte of the Plant, or much lefs altered than in the former Cafe; though the Water will not be fo fharp and penetrating. After this is drawn off, a tartifh, limpid, inodorous Liquor will come over.

And thus may fimple Waters be made fit for long keeping without fpoiling; the Proportion of inflammable Spirit generated in the Fermentation, ferving excellently to preferve them.

CHAP. V.

Of the Simple Waters commonly in Ufe.

SIMPLE Waters are not fo much ufed at prefent as they were formerly; and perhaps one Reafon for their being ne-glected, is the bad Methods ufed in diftilling them; the Procefs is carried on in the fame manner with every Herb; though fome fhould be gently dried, and others diftilled green; fome fhould be drawn with the cold, and others with the hot Still.

The general Rule that fhould be obferved with regard to the hot Still is, that all Herbs fhould have twice their Weight of Water
added

added to them in the Still; and not above a fourth, or a sixth Part of it drawn off again; for simple Waters have their Faints, if drawn too low, as well as those that are spirituous.

Some Plants, particularly Balm, require to have the Water drawn from them cohobated, or poured several times on a fresh Parcel of the Herb, in order to give it a proper Degree of Strength or Richness. Others, on the contrary, abound too much with an essential Oil that floats on the distilled Water; in this case all the Oil should be carefully taken off. Lastly, those that contain a more fixed Oil, should be imperfectly fermented, in the manner laid down in the preceding Chapter, before they are distilled; of this Kind are Carduus, Chamomile, &c.

The simple Waters now commonly made, are Orange-flower-water, Rose-water, Cinnamon-water, Fennel-water, Pepper-mint-water, Spear-mint-water, Balm-water, Pennyroyal-water, *Jamaica* Pepper-water, Castor-water, Simple-water of Orange-peel, and of Dill seed.

CHAP.

CHAP. VI.

Of Orange flower-water.

THE Orange-tree grows plentifully in *Italy*, *Spain*, and *Portugal*, and bears Flowers and Fruit all the Year; but the Fruit is gathered chiefly in *October* and *November*.

The Flowers grow on the younger Shoots among the Leaves: They are white, and conſiſt of a ſingle cup-faſhioned Leaf, cut into five Parts, with ſeveral yellow Stamina in the middle, and of a fragrant odoriferous Smell.

Some Degree of Attention is requiſite to draw a ſimple and odoriferous Water for the Orange Flowers; the Fire muſt be carefully regulated; for too ſmall a Degree will not bring over the eſſential Oil of the Flowers, in which their odoriferous Flavour conſiſts: and, on the contrary, too ſtrong a Fire deſtroys the Fragrancy of the Water, and is very apt to ſcorch the Flowers, and give the Water an empyreumatic Smell. Care ſhould alſo be taken to faſten the Receiver to the End of the Worm with a Bladder, to prevent the volatile Parts from evaporating. The Quantity of Water, alſo, ſhould be

carefully

carefully attended to, if you hope to succeed in the Operation. The following Receipts will answer the Intention.

Receipt for Orange-flower-water.

Take twelve Pounds of Orange-flowers, and twenty-four Quarts of Water, and draw over three Pints.

Or,

Take twelve Pounds of Orange Flowers, and sixteen Quarts of Water; draw over fifteen Quarts, carefully observing what has been observed at the beginning of the Chapter with regard to the Regulation of the Fire.

The Manner of making Double Orange-flower-water, and the essential Oil, or Quintessence of Orange Flowers.

Having shewn how to make simple Orange-flower-water, we shall now shew how to make double Orange-flower-water, and the essential Oil, or Quintessence of Orange Flowers.

Double Orange-flower-water is made, by distilling the Orange Flowers in a cold Still; in the Manner laid down in the first Chapter. The Water extracted in this manner will be very odoriferous and grateful;

ful ; being what is called Double Orange-flower-water. The ſame odoriferous Water will be obtained by diſtilling the Flowers in *Balneum Mariæ*, without any Water in the Still. If the cold Still be uſed put into it as many Flowers as the Head will well cover ; and then make a gentle Fire under the Plate, and as ſoon as you perceive the Still is beginning to work, faſten the Receiver to the Beak of the Still with a Bladder. The ſame Caution muſt be obſerved if the Flowers are diſtilled in *Balneum Mariæ.*

To make this Water to Perfection, the Flowers ſhould be freſh gathered in the Morning with the Dew upon them, if poſſible ; and carefully picked from the Leaves. You ſhould likewiſe make Choice of the largeſt Flowers, becauſe theſe yield moſt in Diſtillation. The Fire muſt be briſk when the Flowers are diſtilled in *Balneum Mariæ*; becauſe the Operation is longer in performing than by the common Alembic, and the Flowers are not here in Danger of being burnt at the Bottom of the Cucurbit. If you would have your Water of a fine Smell, let it be cohobated on freſh Flowers.

With this double Water, the eſſential Oil or Quinteſſence will come over, and float on the Surface of the Water. But a

K   much

much larger Quantity of it will be obtained, by cohobating the Water on fresh Flowers in *Balneum Mariæ*. The essential Oil is at first of a green Colour, but after some Days it will turn reddish. The essential Oil is easily separated from the Water, by the separating Glass, in the following manner: Stop the Spout of the separating Glass with a Cork, and then fill it with the Orange-flower-water; when it has stood a small time the Oil will float on the Surface. Then pull out the Cork, and let the Water run out at the Spout into another Receiver placed for that Purpose. As the Water runs out at the Spout of the Separating-glass, let it be supplied at the Mouth, that the Separating-glass may be always full of Water, till the whole is in this manner poured into it. Then by gently inclining the Glass, pour out all the Water in it through the Spout, and the Oil will remain in the Separating-glass, and may be poured into another Bottle, and kept separate from the Water. The double Orange-flower water is odoriferous; but the essential Oil much more so.

Orange-flower-water is not at present so much used as formerly; but as it is a very odoriferous Water, I thought the Method of making it would be not unaccceptable to the young Distiller.

The

The effential Oil, or Quinteffence of Orange-flowers will make a very grateful Cordial, by mixing it with a clean proof Spirit: The Method of mixing it is this:

Take fome fine Loaf Sugar, and drop on it the Quantity of Oil you intend to diffolve in the Spirit, and rub them well together in a Glafs Mortar, which is what the Chemifts call making an Oleofaccharum. Put this Oleofaccharum into the Spirit; mix them well together, and dulcify it with Sugar to your Tafte. If the Spirit be too ftrong, it may be lowered with Water; but you muft obferve, that if you add Water enough to bring the Spirit confiderably below Proof, it will turn milky; and in order to render it fine, you muft filtrate it thro' thick Flannel, or thin Paper. Twenty Drops of the effential Oil will be fufficient for a Pint of Spirit, and the fame Proportion to a larger Quantity.

CHAP. VII.

Of Rofe-water.

THE Damafk Rofe is the Species intended to be ufed in this Operation; it is of a very fragrant Smell, and flowers in *June* and *July*. The Water may

K 2 be

be made either by the hot Still, the cold Still, or the *Balneum Mariæ*. If the hot Still be uſed, the Leaves picked from the Stalks muſt be put into the Still with a ſufficient Quantity of Water to prevent an Empyreuma, and the Water drawn off by a gentle Fire. The Receiver muſt be luted with a Bladder to the Noſe of the Worm, to prevent the fineſt and moſt volatile Parts from evaporating, which they would otherwiſe do, to the great Prejudice of the Water.

If the cold Still be uſed, the Roſe Leaves either with the Dew on them, or ſprinkled with Water, muſt be laid on the Iron Plate, and covered with the conical Head. A gentle Fire muſt then be made under the Plate, and a Receiver luted with a Bladder to the Noſe of the Still. The Water will gradually diſtil into the Receiver, and be ſtrongly impregnated with the odoriferous Parts of the Roſes.

The ſame Method with regard to the *Balneum Mariæ* muſt be uſed in the Diſtillation of Roſes as in that of Orange-flowers, and therefore need not be repeated here. We ſhall therefore only obſerve, that Roſe-water drawn either by the cold Still, or the *Balneum Mariæ*, is much preferable to that drawn by the hot Still.

The

The Effence, or effential Oil of Rofes is looked upon as one of the moft valuable Perfumes in the World; but at the fame Time the moft difficult to be procured in any Quantity. A fmall Quantity of it is made in *Italy*, but it has always been thought impoffible to procure it here; and, therefore, a Method of acquiring this valuable Commodity will not, I prefume, be difagreeable to the Reader.

Take a Quantity of Damafk Rofe Leaves, put them into a proper Veffel, with a fufficient Quantity of Water, adding fome mineral Acid, as Spirit of Salt, Vitriol, &c. In this Menftruum let the Rofes be digefted for fifteen Days; after which put the Whole into an Alembic, and draw off the Water with a pretty brifk Fire. But, inftead of the common Receiver, a Separating-Glafs muft be placed under the Nofe of the Worm, and a Receiver added to the Tube of the Separating-Glafs. By this Means all the Oil or Effence will float on the Surface of the Water in the Separating-Glafs, and may eafily be feparated from it, when the Operation is finifhed.

K 3 CHAP.

CHAP. VIII.

Of Cinnamon-water.

CInnamon is a thin fine Bark, rolled up in a sort of little Pipes, from the thickness of a Goose-quill, to that of a Man's Thumb, and sometimes more, and about two or three Feet long. Its Colour brownish, with a Mixture of red. It is of an extremely aromatic Smell, and of an acrid and pungent, but very agreeable Taste. It is the interior, or second Bark of a Tree that grows plentifully in *Ceylon.* The People who gather it take off the two Barks together, and immediately separating the outer one, which is rough, and has very little Fragrancy, they lay the other to dry in the Shade in an airy Place, where it rolls itself up into the Form wherein we see it.

The greatest Cheats in the Sale of Cinnamon, are the selling such as has already had its essential Oil distilled from it, and dried again, and the imposing Cassia Lignea in its Place. The first of these is discovered by the want of Pungency in the Cinnamon; the second by this, that the Cassia, when held a little Time in the Mouth, becomes mucilaginous, which the true Cinnamon never does. Cinnamon is a noble Drug, endued

dued with many capital Virtues; it ftrengthens the Vifcera, affifts Concoction, difpels Flatulencies, and is a pleafant Cardiac.

Recipe for one Gallon of fimple Cinnamon-Water.

Take a Pound of the beft Cinnamon grofly powdered, digeft for twenty-four Hours, in two Gallons of Water; put the Whole into an Alembic, and draw over one Gallon with a pretty brifk Fire.

The Oil of Cinnamon, in which the fpecific Virtue of the Drug confifts, is very ponderous, and therefore will not come over the Helm unlefs the Fire be pretty brifk, efpecially with a fimple Water. It will therefore be in vain to attempt diftilling fimple Cinnamon-water by the *Balneum Mariæ.*

CHAP. IX.

Of Fennel-water.

FEnnel-water is extracted from a Seed larger and more beautiful than that produced by our common Fennel; it is called *Sweet Fennel feed,* being of a fragrant Smell, and aromatic fweet Tafte, and is cultivated in *France* and *Italy.* It is to be chofen new, large and fair; but when damp or dufty to be rejected.   K 4   *Recipe*

Recipe for one Gallon of Fennel-water.

Take one Pound of Sweet Fennel-seeds, and two Gallons of Water; put them into an Alembic, and draw off one Gallon with a gentle Fire.

CHAP. X.

Of Pepper-mint-water.

PEpper-mint is a very celebrated Stomachic, and on that account greatly used at present, and its Simple Water often called for.

Recipe for a Gallon of Pepper-mint-water.

Take of the Leaves of dried Pepper-mint, one Pound and a half; Water two Gallons and a half; put all into an Alembic, and draw off one Gallon, with a gentle Fire.

The Water obtained from Pepper-mint by Distillation in *Balneum Mariæ*, is more fragrant and more fully impregnated with the Virtues of the Plant than that drawn by the Alembic. The same may be said with regard to that extracted by the cold Still; when the cold Still is used the Plant must be green, and if possible committed to the still with the Morning Dew upon it.

CHAP.

CHAP. XI.

Of Spear-mint-water.

SPear-mint is alfo like Pepper-mint a great Stomachic, and therefore conftantly ufed.

Recipe for one Gallon of Spear-mint-water.

Take of the Leaves of dried Spear-mint one Pound and a half; Water two Gallons and a half; draw off by a gentle Fire one Gallon.

This Water, like that drawn from Pepper-mint, will be more fragrant if diftilled in *Balneum Mariæ,* or the cold Still; but if the latter be ufed, the fame Caution muft be obferved of diftilling the Plant green.

CHAP. XII.

Of Baum-water.

BAUM is a Plant well known in our Gardens. It flowers in *July,* and is of a fine cordial Flavour; but fo weak, that it is foon diffipated and loft; nor is it eafy to dry it fo as to preferve its natural Scent.

Baum-

Baum-water, therefore should be drawn when the Plant is green; and in order to procure the Water in full Perfection, it should be cohobated, or returned several times upon fresh Parcels of the Plant; by this means a Water may be procured from Baum extremely rich, and of considerable Use as a Cordial.

If the *Balneum Mariæ* be used, the Water is much better than that drawn by an Alembic. The Water drawn from this Plant by the cold Still will also be very fragrant, and highly impregnated with the Virtues of the Plant.

C H A P. XIII.

Of Penny-royal-water.

PEnny-royal, a Plant very common in *England*, is very warm, and its Parts very subtile and penetrating: It is one of the first Plants in Esteem in the present Practice, as well as in former Ages, as an Attenuant and Uterine. It is good in Flatulences and Suppressions of Urine, and by many is greatly recommended in Dropsies, Jaundices, and other chronic Distempers. It communicates its Virtues to Water in Infusion, and its simple Water has, perhaps,

more

more Virtue than any other kept in the Shops. But as it is requiſite in order to obtain a Water fully impregnated with the Virtues of Baum, to cohobate it on freſh Parcels of the Plant; the Water drawn from green Penny-royal, on the contrary, generally contains ſo large a Portion of the eſſential Oil, that it is neceſſary to ſeparate what floats on the Surface of the Water, by the Separating-glaſs.

Recipe for one Gallon of Penny-royal-water.

Take of the dried Leaves of Penny-royal one Pound and a half, of Water three Gallons; draw off one Gallon with a gentle Fire.

The Water drawn from green Penny-royal by the cold Still, is very fragrant, and fully impregnated with the Virtues of the Plant.

CHAP. XIV.

Of Jamaica-*Pepper-water.*

*J*Amaica-Pepper, or Pimento, is the Fruit of a tall Tree growing in the mountainous Parts of *Jamaica*, where it is much cultivated, becauſe of the great Profit ariſing from the cured Fruit, ſent in large Quantities annually into *Europe.*

it

It is gathered, when green, and expoſed to the Sun for many Days on Clóths, and frequently ſhaked and turned, till thoroughly dry; great Care is taken during the Time of drying to defend the Fruit from the Morning and Evening Dews; when thoroughly dried it is ſent over to us.

It is a very noble Aromatic, and deſerves to be uſed more frequently than it is at preſent. The ſimple Water drawn from it is a better Carminative than any other ſimple Water at preſent in uſe.

Recipe for a Gallon of Jamaica-Pepper-water.

Take of *Jamaica* Pepper half a Pound, Water two Gallons and a half; draw off one Gallon, with a pretty briſk Fire. The Oil of this Fruit is very ponderous, and therefore this Water is beſt made in an Alembic.

CHAP. XV.

Of Caſtor-water.

THIS Drug is brought to us in the Pods or Bags that naturally contained it, and theſe ſo much reſemble the Teſticles

of

of an Animal, both in their dry State, and when on the Body of the Creatures, that it is no wonder People who did not examine their Situation on the Animal, really took them for ſuch ; it is, however, a peculiar ſecreted Matter, contained in Bags deſtined, to receive it.

Caſtor is an indurated Subſtance, formed of a Matter once fluid ; the thinner Part of which has been evaporated by drying. It is a light and friable Matter, of a moderately. lax Texture, and of a deep duſky brown Colour. It is of a ſomewhat acrid and bit-teriſh Taſte, and of a ſtrong fœtid Smell, which, to many, is very diſagreeable.

The Animal that produces the Caſtor is by all Authors called Caſtor and Fiber, and by the Vulgar, the Beaver.

The Caſtor of ſeveral Parts of the World differs in Goodneſs, and in regard to the Care taken in the drying. The *Ruſſian* Caſtor has long been the moſt eſteemed, and the *New England* kind the leaſt.

Caſtor-water is of great Uſe in hyſteric Caſes, and all Diſeaſes of the Nerves ; in Epilepſies, Palſies, and all Complaints of that kind.

Recipe

Recipe for making one Gallon of Castor-water.

Take of *Russia* Castor an Ounce, of Water three Gallons; draw off one Gallon with a pretty brisk Fire.

C H A P. XVI.

Of Orange-peel-water.

THE Orange is a Fruit too well known to need a Description here. The Water is very grateful to the Taste, and often used in Fevers, &c.

Recipe for one Gallon of Orange-peel-water.

Take of the outward yellow Rind of *Seville* Oranges, four Ounces; Water three Gallons and a half; draw off one Gallon by the Alembic, with a pretty brisk Fire.

C H A P. XVII.

Of the Water of Dill-seed.

DILL greatly resembles Fennel both in Root, Stalk, or Leaf, but rarely grows so tall, or is so much branched; it bears the same kind of yellow Umbels of Flowers, after which come Seeds rounder, broader,

·and

and flatter than thofe of Fennel. The whole Plant is of a ftrong Scent, lefs pleafant than Fennel. It grows in Gardens, and flowers and feeds in *July* and *Auguft*. The Water drawn from the Seeds is heating and carminative, good in Cholics, and all Diforders arifing from Wind.

Recipe for making a Gallon of the Water of Dill-feed.

Take of Dill-feed one Pound, Water three Gallons; diftil off by the Alembic one Gallon, with a pretty brifk Fire.

The Waters we have enumerated in this Part are thofe now commonly in ufe; though there are many other Herbs, from whence Waters of great Ufe may be drawn; but as the Method of Diftillation is the fame in all, it would be of no Ufe to extend thefe Inftructions to a greater length; we fhall therefore only obferve, that when unfavourable Seafons have prevented the Herbs from attaining a proper Degree of Perfection, it will be neceffary to increafe their Proportion in extracting the feveral Waters ordered to be drawn by the Alembic.

A

A

Complete System

OF

DISTILLATION.

PART III.

Of making compound Waters and Cordials.

THE Perfection of this grand Branch of Distillery depends upon the Observation of the following general Rules, easy to be observed and practised.

L   I.

1. The Artift muft always be careful to ufe a well cleanfed Spirit, or one freed from its own effential Oil, as were before obferved, Part I. Chap. xxiii. For as a compound Water is nothing more than a Spirit impregnated with the effential Oil of the Ingredients, it is neceffary that the Spirit fhould have depofited its own.

2. Let the Time of previous Digeftion be proportioned to the Tenacity of the Ingredients, or the Ponderofity of their Oil. Thus Cloves and Cinnamon require a longer Digeftion before they are diftilled than Calamus Aromaticus or Orange-peel. Sometimes Cohobation (explained in Part II. Chap. iii.) is neceffary; for Inftance, in making the ftrong Cinnamon-water; becaufe the effential Oil of Cinnamon is fo extremely ponderous, that it is difficult to bring it over the Helm with the Spirit without Cohobation.

3. Let the Strength of the Fire be proportioned to the Ponderofity of the Oil intended to be raifed with the Spirit. Thus, for Inftance, the ftrong Cinnamon Water requires a much greater Degree of Fire than that from lax Vegetables, as Mint, Baum, &c.

4. Let only a due Proportion of the fineft Parts of the effential Oil be united with the Spirit; the groffer and lefs fragrant Parts of the Oil not giving the Spirit fo agreeable a Flavour, and at the fame Time renders it thick and unfightly. This may in a great Meafure be effected by leaving out the Faints, and making up to Proof with fine foft Water in their ftead.

Thefe four Rules carefully obferved will render this extenfive Part of Diftillation far more perfect than it is at prefent. Nor will their be any Occafion for the ufe of burnt Allum, White of Eggs, Ifinglafs, &c. to fine down Cordial Waters; for they will prefently be fine, fweet and pleafant tafted; without any farther Trouble.

C H A P. I.

Of ftrong Cinnamon Water.

W E have already (Chap. viii. Part II.) defcribed this Drug, and given fome Directions for chufing the beft Sort, to which the Reader is refered.

Caffia Buds are in general Recipe in the infufion cinnamon water & give a Much finer flavour —

Recipe for sixteen Gallons of strong Cinnamon Water.

Take eight Pounds of fine Cinnamon bruised, seventeen Gallons of clean rectified Spirit, and two Gallons of Water. Put them into your Still, and digest them twenty-four Hours with a gentle Heat; after which draw off sixteen Gallons by a pretty strong Heat.

I have ordered a much larger Quantity of Cinnamon than is common among Distillers, because when made in the Manner above directed, it is justly looked upon as one of the noblest Cordial Waters of the Shops; but when made in the common Way of two Pounds to twenty Gallons of Spirit, as some have ordered, is only an Imposition on the Buyer. Some also, to render the Goods cheaper, use equal Quanties of Cinnamon and Cassia Lignea; but by this means the Cordial is rendered much worse; and, therefore, if you desire a fine Cinnamon-water the above Recipe will answer your Intention: But if a cheaper Sort be desired you may lessen the Quantity of Cinnamon, and add Cassia Lignea in its stead. If you would dulcify your Cinnamon-water, take double refined Sugar, what Quantity you please, the general Pro-

portion

portion is, about two Pounds to a Gallon, and diſſolve it in the Spirit after you have made it up Proof with clean Water. One general Caution is here neceſſary to be added; namely, that near the End of the Operation you carefully watch the Spirit as it runs into the Receiver, in order to prevent the Faints mixing with the Goods. This you may diſcover by often catching ſome of it, as it runs from the Worm in a Glaſs, and obſerving whether it is fine and tranſparent; for as ſoon as ever the Faints begin to riſe, the Spirit will have an azure or bluiſh Caſt. As ſoon therefore as you perceive this Alteration, change the Receiver immediately; for if you ſuffer the Faints to mix with your other Goods, the Value of the whole will be greatly leſſened. With regard to the Faints, they are to be kept by themſelves, and poured into the Still when a freſh Parcel of the ſame Goods is to be made.

It is alſo neceſſary to obſerve here, once for all, that the Diſtillers call all Goods made up Proof, *double Goods*; and thoſe which are below Proof, *ſingle*. This Obſervation will be alone ſufficient to inſtruct the young Diſtiller, how he may at any Time turn his Proof or double Goods into ſingle.

L 3 CHAP.

CHAP. II.

Of Clove Water.

CLOVES, from whence this Water takes its Name, are the Fruit of a Tree growing in the *Molucca* Islands. The Figure of this Fruit is oblong, and not very thick, resembling in some measure, a Nail. The Surface of it is rough, and the Colour a dusky brown with an admixture of reddish. The whole Fruit is of an extremely fragant Smell, and of an acrid, pungent, and very aromatic Taste. Cloves are to be chosen the largest, fairest, darkest coloured, the heaviest and most unctuous on the Surface, when pressed between the Fingers. Cloves are carminative, and good against all Distempers of the Head arising from cold Causes. They strengthen the Sight, and are good against Faintings, Palpitations of the Heart, and Crudities in the Stomach.

Recipe for fifteen Gallons of Clove Water.

Take of Cloves bruised four Pounds, Pimento or All-spice half a Pound, clean Proof of Spirit sixteen Gallons; let it digest twelve Hours in a gentle Heat, and then

draw

draw off fifteen Gallons with a pretty brifk Fire.

Or,

Take *Winter*'s Bark, four Pounds, Pimento fix Ounces, Cloves one Pound and a Quarter; clean Proof Spirits fixteen Gallons: Digeft, and draw off as before.

The *Winter*'s Bark, added in the fecond Recipe is the Bark of a large Tree, growing in feveral Parts of *America*, and has its name from its Difcoverer Captain *Winter*. The outer Rind of it is of an uneven Surface, and of a loofe Texture, very brittle, and eafily powdered. The inner Part, in which the principal Virtue refides, is hard, and of a dufky reddifh brown Colour. It is of an extremely fragant and aromatic Smell, and of a fharp, pungent, and fpicy Tafte, much hotter than Cinnamon in the Mouth, and leaving in it a more lafting Flavour. It is to be chofen in Pieces not too large, having the inner or brown Part firm and found, and of a very pungent Tafte. It is apt to be worm-eaten; but in that Cafe it fhould be wholly rejected, as having loft the moft effential Part of its Virtue.

If you defire to have your Clove Water red, it may be coloured either by a ftrong Tincture of Cochineal, Alkanet-root, or

L 4   Corn-

Corn-poppy-flowers. The firſt gives the moſt elegant Colour, but it is not often uſed on Account of its Dearneſs.

You may dulcify it to your Palate, by diſſolving in it double refined Sugar. Some for Cheapneſs uſe a coarſer Kind of Sugar; but this renders the Goods foul and unſightly. Some alſo, to ſave Expences, make what they call Clove Water, with Cloves and Caraway-ſeeds; the Proportion they generally uſe is half an Ounce of Cloves, and two Drams of Carraway-ſeeds to a Gallon of Spirit.

C H A P. III.

Of Lemon Water.

THE Peel of the Lemon, the Part uſed in making this Water, is a very grateful bitter Aromatic, and on that Account very ſerviceable in repairing and ſtrengthening the Stomach.

Recipe for ten Gallons of Lemon Water.

Take of dried Lemon-peel four Pounds, clean Proof Spirit ten Gallons and a Half, and one Gallon of Water. Draw off ten Gallons by a gentle Fire. Some dulcify

Lemon-

Lemon-water, but by that means its Virtues as a Stomachic, are greatly impaired.

CHAP. IV.

Of Hungary Water.

ROSEMARY, the principal Ingredient in Hungary Water, has always been a favourite Shrub in Medicine; it is full of volatile Parts, as appears by its Taſte and Smell. It is a very valuable Cephalic, and is good in all Diſorders of the Nerves; in Hyſteric and Hypocodriac Caſes, in Palſies, Apoplexies, and Vertigoes. Some ſuppoſe that the Flowers poſſeſs the Virtues of the whole Plant in a more exalted Degree than any other Part; but the flowery Tops, Leaves, and Huſks, together with the Flowers themſelves, are much fitter for all Purpoſes, than the Flowers alone.

Recipe for ten Gallons of Hungary Water.

Take of the flowery Tops, with the Leaves and Flowers of Roſemary fourteen Pounds, rectified Spirit eleven Gallons and a Half, Water one Gallon, diſtil off ten Gallons with a moderate Fire. If you perform this Operation in Balneum Mariæ, your Hungary Water will be much finer, than if drawn by the common Alembic.

This

This is called Hungary Water, from its being firſt made for a Princeſs of that King-dom. Some add Lavender-flowers, and others Florentine-orice-root; but what is moſt eſteemed is made with Roſemary only.

CHAP. V.

Of Lavender Water.

THERE are two Sorts of Lavender Water, the Simple and Compound; the firſt is much uſed externally on Account of its Fragrancy, and cephalic Virtues; the latter internally in a great Number of Diſ-orders.

Recipe for ten Gallons of ſimple Lavender Water.

Take fourteen Pounds of Lavender-flowers, ten Gallons and a Half of rec-tified Spirit of Wine, and one Gallon of Water; draw off ten Gallons with a gentle Fire; or, which is much better, in Bal-neum Mariæ.

Both the Hungary and Lavender Water, may be made at any Time of the Year without Diſtillation, by mixing the Oil of the Plant with highly rectified Spirit of Wine.

Wine. In order to this, when the Plant is in Perfection, you ſhould diſtill a large Quantity of it in Water with a very briſk Fire; placing under the Noſe of the Worm the Separating-glaſs (deſcribed Page 31. Part I. of this Treatiſe) by which means you will obtain the eſſential Oil of the Plant, in which both its Fragrancy and Virtues reſide. Having procured the eſſential Oil of the Plant, the Water may readily be made in the following Manner. Put the rectified Spirit into the Receiver (deſcribed Page 32. Fig. xii.) and let an Aſſiſtant ſhake it with a quick Motion; whilſt the Spirit is thus agitated, drop in leiſurely the eſſential Oil, and it will mix without any Foulneſs or Milkineſs. The Oils of Lavender and Roſemary are imported cheaper from abroad, than they can be made here; but theſe Oils will not mix with the Spirit, without rendering it foul and milky; and therefore if you propoſe making Hungary or Lavender Water in this Manner; it will be neceſſary to extract the Oil yourſelf.

Recipe for making three Gallons of compound Lavender Water.

Take of Lavender Water above deſcribed two Gallons, of Hungary Water one Gallon, Cinnamon and Nutmegs of each three Ounces, and of red Saunders one Ounce; digeſt

digeſt the whole three Days in a gentle Heat, and then filter it for uſe. Some add Saffron, Muſk, and Ambergreaſe of each half a Scruple; but theſe are now generally omitted.

This compound Lavender Water has been long celebrated in all nervous Caſes. In all Kinds of Palſies, and Loſs of Memory it is of the greateſt Service; and has been ſo much remarked for its Efficacy in theſe Complaints, as almoſt univerſally to obtain the Name of *Palſy Drops.*

CHAP. VI.

Of Citron Water.

THE Citron is an agreeable Fruit reſembling a Lemon in Colour, Smell and Taſte. The Inſide is white, fleſhy and thick, containing but a ſmall Quantity of Pulp, in Proportion to the Bigneſs of the Fruit.

Recipe for making ten Gallons of Citron Water.

Take of dry yellow Rinds of Citron four Pounds, clean Proof Spirit ten Gallons and a Half, Water one Gallon, digeſt the whole twenty-four Hours with a gently Heat;

draw

draw off ten Gallons, with a gentle Fire; or, which is much better, in Balneum Mariæ, and dulcify it with fine Sugar to your Palate.

Or,

Take of dry yellow Rinds of Citrons three Pounds, of Orange-peel two Pounds, Nutmegs bruifed three Quarters of a Pound; digeft, draw off, and dulcify as before.

This is one of the moft pleafant Cordials we have; and the Addition of the Nutmegs, in the fecond Receipt, increafes its Virtue as a Cephalic and Stomachic.

CHAP. VII.

Of Anifeed Water.

ANISEED is a fmall Seed of an oblong Shape, each way ending in an obtufe Point; its Surface is very deeply ftriated, and it is of a foft and lax Subftance, very light and eafily broken. Its colour is a Kind of pale olive, or greenifh grey; it has a very ftrong and aromatic Smell, and a fweetifh but acrid Tafte, but in the whole not difagreeable. Anifeed fhould be chofen large, fair, new, and clean, of a good Smell, and acrid Tafte. The Plant that produces it is cultivated in many Parts of *France*; but the fineft Seed comes from
the

the Island of *Malta*, where it is raised for Sale, and whence a great Part of *Europe* is supplied.

Recipe for ten Gallons of Aniseed Water.

Take of Aniseed bruised two Pounds; Proof Spirits twelve Gallons and a Half; Water one Gallon; draw off ten Gallons with a moderate Fire.

Or,

Take of the Seeds of Anise and Angelica, each two Pounds, Proof Spirits twelve Gallons and a half; draw off as before.

Aniseed Water should never be reduced below Proof, because of the large Quantity of Oil with which the Spirit is impregnated, and which will render the Goods milky and foul, when brought down below Proof; but if there be a necessity for doing this, the Goods must be filtrated either thro' Paper or the filtrating Bag, which will restore their Transparency.

Aniseed Water is a good Carminative, and therefore in great Request among the common People against the Cholic.

C H A P.

C H A P. VIII.

Of Caraway Water.

CARAWAY-SEED is of an oblong and ſlender Figure, pointed at both Ends, and thickeſt in the Middle. It is ſtriated on the Surface, conſiderably heavy, of a deep brown Colour, and ſomewhat bright or gloſſy. It is of a very penetrating Smell, not diſagreeable, and of a hot, acrid and bitteriſh Taſte. Caraway-ſeed is to be choſen large, new and of a good Colour, not duſty, and of an agreeable Smell. The Plant which produces the Caraway-ſeed grows wild in the Meadows of *France* and *Italy*, and in many other Places; but is ſown in Fields for the ſake of the Seeds in *Germany*, and many other Parts of *Europe*.

Recipe for making ten Gallons of Caraway Water.

Take of Caraway-ſeeds bruiſed three Pounds, Proof Spirit twelve Gallons, Water two Gallons; draw off ten Gallons, or till the Faints begin to riſe; make the Goods up with clean Water, and dulcify with common Sugar to your Taſte.

Or,

Or,

Take of Caraway-feed bruifed two Pounds and a Half, Orange or Lemon-peel dried one Pound, Proof Spirit twelve Gallons, Water two Gallons; draw off and dulcify as before.

Caraway Water, like that of Anifeed, is a good Carminative; but not fo much ufed, tho' much pleafanter.

CHAP. IX.

Of Cardamom Seed Water.

THE Seed from whence this Water takes its Name, is called by Botanifts *Cardamum Minus*, or the leffer Cardamom; to diftinguifh it from the *Cardamomum Majus*, or Grains of Paradife.

The leffer Cardamom is a fmall fhort Fruit, or membranaceous Capfule, of a trigonal Form, about a third of an Inch long, and fwelling out thick about the Middle; beginning fmall and narrow from the Stalk, and terminating in a fmall, but obtufe Point at the End. It is ftriated all over very deeply with longitudinal Furrows, and confifts of a thin but very tough Membrane, of a fibrous Texture, and pale-brown

brown Colour, with a faint Caſt of red. When the Fruit is thoroughly ripe, this Membrane opens at the three Edges all the way, and ſhews that it is internally divided by three thin Membranes into three Cells, in each of which is an Arrangement of Seeds, ſeparately lodged in two Series. The Seeds are of an irregular angular Figure, rough, and of a duſky brown Colour on the Surface, with a Mixture of yellowiſh and reddiſh, and of white Colour within. They have not much Smell, unleſs firſt bruiſed, when they are much like Camphire under the Noſe. They are of an acrid, aromatic and firey hot Taſte. They ſhould be choſen ſound, cloſe ſhut on all Sides, and full of Seeds, of a good Smell, and of an acrid aromatic Taſte.

Recipe for ten Gallons of Cardamom Seed Water.

Take of the leſſer Cardamom Seeds huſked two Pounds and a Half, of clean Proof Spirit ten Gallons and a Half, and of Water one Gallon; draw off ten Gallons by a gentle Heat. You may either dulcify it or not with fine Sugar at pleaſure.

This Water is Carminative, aſſiſts Digeſtion, and good to ſtrengthen the Head and Stomach.

M   C H A P.

CHAP. X.

Of Aqua Mirabilis; or, the Wonderful-Water.

MOST of the Ingredients in this Composition have already been described, and an Account of the Nutmegs will be given in Chap. xxv. But the Cubebs and Ginger remain to be mentioned.

Cubebs are small dried Fruit resembling a Pepper-corn, but often somewhat longer; of a dark brown Colour, composed of a wrinkled external Bark; of an aromatic, tho' not very strong Smell, and of an acrid and pungent Taste, tho' less so than Pepper; but its Acrimony continues long on the Tongue, and draws forth a large Quantity of Saliva. We have two Kinds of Cubebs, which differ only in their Periods of gathering, both are produced from the same Plant. The unripe Cubebs are small, very wrinkled on the Surface, and their Nucleus, when broken, is flacid: But the ripe ones not so. Cubebs are brought from the Island *Java*, where they grow in great Abundance. They should be chosen large, fresh, and sound, and the heaviest possible. They are warm and carminative, and e-
esteemed

fteemed good in Vertigoes, Palfies, and Diforders of the Stomach.

Ginger is a Root too well known to need a long Defcription; it is fufficient to ob- ferve that it is of a pale yellowifh Colour when broken, of a fibrous Structure, and eafily beat into a Sort of woolly or long thready Matter. It is of very hot, acrid, and very pungent Tafte; but Aromatic withal, and of a very agreeable Smell. We have it both from the *Eaft* and *Weft Indies*; but the oriental is much fup- perior to the occidental in its Flavour, of a firmer Subftance, and does not beat out fo much into Threads. Ginger is an excellent Carminative and Stomachic; it affifts Digef- tion, difpells Flatus's, and takes off Cholic Pains almoft inftantaneoufly.

There are feveral Receipts for making this celebrated Cordial; but the following are allowed to be the beft.

Take of Cinnamon one Pound and a Quarter, Rind of Lemon-peels ten Ounces, Cubebs one Ounce and a Quarter, Leaves of Baum one Pound; bruife all thefe In- gredients, and pour on them eleven Gal- lons of clean Proof Spirit, and one Gallon of Water; digeft the whole twenty-four Hours, and diftil off ten Gallons with a

M 2 pretty

pretty brisk Fire; and dulcify it with fine Sugar.

Or,

Take of the lesser Cardamoms, Cloves, Cubebs, Galangal, Mace, Nutmeg, and Ginger, of each one Pound and three Quarters, of the yellow part of Citron-peel and Cinnamon of each three Pounds and a Half, of the Leaves of Balm one Pound; bruise these Ingredients, and pour on them eleven Gallons of Spirit and one Gallon of Water; digest, and draw off, &c. as before.

This Cordial has been long celebrated as a noble Stomachic, and therefore greatly called for.

Some instead of all the Ingredients enumerated in the above Receipts use only Pimento; and this is the sort of **Aqua Mirabilis** which some sell so very cheap.

C H A P. XI.

Of Mint Water.

THE Mint intended in this Recipe is the common Spear-mint, an Account of which has already been given. Page 137.

Page 137.

Recipe

Recipe for ten Gallons of Mint Water.

Take of dry Spear-mint Leaves fourteen Pounds, Proof Spirit ten Gallons and a Half, Water two Gallons; draw off ten Gallons by a gentle Heat. You may dulcify it with Sugar if required.

Mint Water is greatly recommended by the learned *Boerhaave* and *Hoffman*, againſt Vomitting, Nauſeas, and the Cholic.

C H A P. XII.

Of Pepper Mint Water.

THE Pepper-mint has been already deſcribed Page 136, to which the Reader is referred.

Recipe for ten Gallons of Pepper Mint Water.

Take of dry Pepper Mint Leaves fourteen Pounds, Proof Spirit ten Gallons and a Half, Water one Gallon; draw off ten Gallons by a gentle Fire. You may either dulcify it or not.

Pepper Mint Water is a noble Stomachic, good againſt Vomiting, Nauſeas, Cholic,

M 3 and

and other griping Pains in the Bowels, in all which Intentions it greatly exceeds the common Spear Mint Water.

C H A P. XIII.

Of *Angelica Water*.

THERE are two Sorts of Angelica Water, the Single and the Compound. I shall give Receipts for making both Kinds; and with regard to the Nature of Angelica, it is sufficient to observe, that it is an excellent Carminative.

Recipe for ten Gallons of single Angelica Water.

Take of the Roots and Seed of Angelica cut and bruised, of each one Pound and a Half, Proof Spirit eleven Gallons, Water two Gallons; draw off ten Gallons, or till the Faints begin to rise, with a gentle Fire; and dulcify it, if required, with lump Sugar.

This Angelica Water is a good Carminative, and therefore good against all Kinds of flatulent Cholics, and Gripings of the Bowels.

Recipe

Recipe for ten Gallons of Compound Angelica Water.

Take of the Roots and Seeds of Angelica, and of fweet Fennel-feeds of each one Pound and a Half, of the dried Leaves of Baum and Sage of each one Pound; flice the Roots and bruife the Seeds and Herbs, and add to them of Cinnamon one Ounce, of Cloves, Cubebs, Galangals, and Mace, of each three Quarters of an Ounce, of Nutmegs, the leffer Cardamom-feed, Pimento, and Saffron of each half an Ounce; infufe all thefe in twelve Gallons of clean Proof Spirit, and draw off ten Gallons, with a pretty brifk Fire. It may be dulcified or not at pleafure.

This is an excellent Compofition, and a powerful Carminative; and good in all flatulent Cholics, and other griping Pains in the Bowels. It is alfo good in Naufeas, and other Diforders of the Stomach.

It may not be amifs to obferve here, that in diftilling this and feveral other Compofitions, abounding with oily Seeds, the Operator fhould be careful not to let the Faints mix with the other Goods, as they would by that means be rendered naufeous and unfightly; he fhould therefore be care-

M 4   ful

ful towards the letter End of the Operation, to catch some of the Spirit as it runs
from the Worm in a Glass; and as soon as
ever he perceives it the least cloudy, to remove the Receiver, and draw the Faints by
themselves.

C H A P. XIV.

Of Orange Water.

THIS Water is made in the same Man-
ner from the Peels of Oranges, as
Citron Water; Chap. vi. is from the Peels of
Citrons.

Recipe for ten Gallons of Orange Water.

Take of the yellow Part of fresh Orange-
peels five Pounds, clean Proof Spirit ten
Gallons and a Half, Water two Gallons;
draw off ten Gallons with a gentle Fire.

This is a good Stomachic, and may also
be used for making bitter Tinctures, as that
called *Stoughton*'s Drops.

CHAP.

CHAP. XV.

Of Plague Water.

THERE are ſeveral Receipts for making Plague Water; but the following are much the beſt.

Recipe for ten Gallons of Plague Water.

Take of the Roots of Maſterwort and Butter-burr, of each one Pound and a Quarter, *Virginia* Snake-root and Zeadory, of each ten Ounces, Angelica-ſeeds and Bay-ſeeds of each fourteen Ounces, and of the Leaves of Scordium one Pound and a Half. Cut or bruiſe theſe Ingredients and put them into the Still, with twelve Gallons of clean Proof Spirit, and two Gallons of Water; digeſt the whole for twenty-four Hours, and draw off ten Gallons.

Or,

Take of the Leaves of Celandine, Roſemary, Rue, Sage, Roman Wormwood, Dragons Agrimony, Baum, Scordium, the leſſer Centory, Carduus Benedictus, Betony, and Mint, of each twenty Handfuls; of dried Angelica-root, Zeadory and Gentian, of each ten Ounces, and of *Virginia* Snak-root five Ounces; digeſt theſe twenty-four Hours, in twelve Gallons of clean Proof Spirit,

Spirit, and two Gallons of Water; and then draw off ten Gallons as before.

Or,

Take of Rue, Rosemary, Baum, Carduus Benedictus, Scordium, Marigold-flowers, Dragons, Goat's-rue, and Mint, of each ten Handfuls; Roots of Masterwort, Angelica, Butter-burr, and Peony, of each one Pound and a Quarter; and of Viper-grass ten Ounces; digest in twelve Gallons of Spirit, &c. as before.

Or,

Take of the Roots of Masterwort, Gentian, and Snake-root, of each seven Ounces; green Walnuts bruised eighty; Venice-treacle and Mithridate of each three Ounces; Camphire six Drams; of the Roots of Rue and Elecampane, of each three Ounces; Hore-hound six Ounces; Saffron six Drams; Proof Spirit twelve Gallons; digest, &c. as before.

Or,

Take Dragons, Rosemary, Wormwood, Sage, Scordium, Mugwort, Scabious, Baum, Carduus, Angelica, Marigold-flowers, Centory, Betony, Pimpernel, Celadine, Rue, and Agrimony, of each three Pounds; of the Roots of Gentian, Zeadory, Liquorice, and Elecampane, of each twelve Ounces; twelve Gallons of Spirits; digest, &c. as before.

Or,

Or,

Take of green Walnuts, five Pounds;
of Angelica-root two Pounds; of the
Leaves of Angelica, Rue, Sage, and Scordium, of each ten Handfuls; of Nutmegs,
Long Pepper, Ginger, Camphire, and Gen-
tian-root, of each five Ounces; of Snake-
root, Contrayerva, Elecampane, Zeadory,
and Viper's Flefh, of each thirteen Ounces;
Venice Treacle and Mithridate of each thirteen Ounces; White-wine Vinegar feven
Pounds; Proof Spirits twelve Gallons; digeft, *&c.* as before.

You may either dulcify your Plague-wa-
ter, or not, as you fee occafion.

All the above Receipts for making Plague
Water are in ufe; but the firft the moft elegant, containing nothing but what is proper in the Intention, and at the fame time
adapted to give its Virtues by Diftillation;
which cannot be faid of any of the reft,
feveral of the Ingredients adding no Virtue at all to the Water. Of this Kind are
the Celandine, Carduus, Centory, Gentian,
Walnuts, *&c.*

Plague Water is a noble Alexipharmic,
and a high Carminative Cordial in malig-
nant Cafes, and of great Ufe in Lownefs
of Spirits, and Depreffions.

CHAP.

C H A P. XVI.

Of Dr. Stephens's *Water.*

THIS Water has its Name from its Inventor, a Physician of great Learning and Practice.

Recipe for ten Gallons of Dr. Stephens's *Water.*

Take of Cinnamon, Ginger, Galangal, Cloves, Nutmegs, Grains of Paradise, the Seeds of Anise, sweet Fennel, and Caraway, of each one Ounce; of the Leaves of Thyme, Mother of Thyme, Mint, Sage, Penniroyal, Rosemary, Flowers of red Roses, Camomile, Origanum, and Lavender, of each eight Handfuls; of clean Proof Spirit twelve Gallons, Water two Gallons; digest all twenty-four Hours, and then draw off ten Gallons, or till the Faints begin to rise. Dulcify with fine Sugar to your Palate.

This is a noble Cephalic Cordial and Carminative; and also in some Degree an Hysteric; good in all cholic Pains in the Stomach and Bowels, and Diseases of the Nerves.

CHAP.

CHAP. XVII.

Of Surfeit Water.

THERE are two Kinds of Surfeit-water, one made by Diftillation, and the other by Infufion, the former is generally called white *Surfeit Water*, and latter red *Surfeit Water*.

Recipe for ten Gallons of white Surfeit Water.

Take Marigold-flowers, Mint, Centory, Rofemary, Scordium, Mugwort, Carduus, Rue, St. John's-wort, Baum, and Dragons, of each feven Handfuls; of the Roots of Peony, Viper-grafs, Butter-burr, and Angelica, of each one Pound and a Half; of Galangal, Calamus Aromaticus, and of the Seeds of Angelica and Caraway, of each four Ounces; of the Flowers of red Poppies ten Handfuls; Proof Spirit twelve Gallons, Water two Gallons; digeft for twenty-four Hours, and then draw off ten Gallons, or till the Faints begin to rife; and dulcify with fine Sugar.

This is a good Cordial, but would not be the worfe, if the Carduus, Mugwort, Rue and St. John's-wort, were omitted, as little

of

of their Virtues can be obtained by Diftillation. It is, however, a good Alexipharmic, Carminative, and Stomachic; and therefore good in all flatulent Pains in the Stomach and Bowels, in Naufeas and Surfeits, from whence it had its Name.

Recipe for making ten Gallons of red Surfeit Water.

Take of the Flowers of red Poppies, two Bufhels, eleven Gallons of clean Proof Spirit, and digeft them with a gentle Heat for three Days, or till the Spirit has extracted all the Colour of the Flowers: Then prefs out the Liquor from the Flowers, and add to the Tincture of the Seeds of Caraway and Coriander, and Liquorice-root fliced, of each ten Ounces; of Cardamoms and Cubebs of each four Ounces; of Raifins ftoned five Pounds; of Cinnamon five Ounces; of Nutmegs, Mace, and Ginger, of each three Ounces; of Cloves two Drams; of Juniper-berries three Ounces; let the whole be digefted three Days, then prefs-out the Liquor adding to it a Gallon of Rofe-water; and then ftrain or filter the whole through a Flannel Bag.

This Water is much Superior to the preceding, as all the Ingredients will give their Virtues to the Tincture, tho' they will not rife in Diftillation. It is a noble Alexipharmic,

pharmic, it ftrengthens the Stomach, and greatly affifts Digeftion ; it is alfo an excellent Carminative and good againft the Cholic and Gripes : Its Cordial Virtues renders it ferviceable in all Tremblings of the Nerves, and Depreffions of the Spirits.

C H A P. XVIII.

Of Wormwood Water.

THERE are two Sorts of Wormwood Water, diftinguifhed by the Epithets of *greater* and *leffer.*

Recipe for making ten Gallons of the leffer Compofition of Wormwood Water.

Take of the Leaves of dried Wormwood five Pounds ; of the leffer Cardamomfeeds five Ounces ; of Coriander-feeds one Pound ; of clean Proof Spirit eleven Gallons ; Water one Gallon ; draw off ten Gallons, or till the Faints begin to rife, with a gentle Fire. It may be dulcified with Sugar, or not, at pleafure.

This is a good Stomachic and Carminative ; and on that Account often called for.

Recipe

*Recipe for ten Gallons of the greater Com-
pofition of Wormwood Water.*

Take of the common and Sea Worm-
wood, dried, of each ten Pounds; of Sage,
Mint, and Baum dried, of each twenty
Handfuls; of the Roots of Galangal,
Ginger, Calamus Aromaticus, and Elecam-
pane; of the Seed of fweet Fennel and
Coriander, of each three Ounces; of Cin-
namon, Cloves, and Nutmegs, the leffer
Cardamoms and Cubebs, of each two
Ounces. Cut and bruife the Ingredients as
they require; digeft them twenty-four
Hours, in eleven Gallons of fine Proof
Spirit, and two Gallons of Water, and draw
off ten Gallons, or till the Faints begin to
rife, with a pretty brifk Fire.

This is an excellent Compofition, and
good in all Difeafes of the Stomach arifing
either from Wind or a bad Digeftion. It
is greatly in ufe in fome Parts of *England*,
but comes too dear for the common Sort
of People; on which account a Cordial
Water is often fold under the Title of *the
greater Compofition of Wormwood Water*; drawn
from the Leaves of Wormwood, Orange
and Lemon-peel, Calamus Aromaticus, Pimento, and the Seeds of Anife and Caraway; which being all cheap Ingredients,

the

the Compoſition may be ſold at a moderate Price. A Water drawn in this manner is a good Carminative; but far inferior to that made by the above Recipe.

CHAP. XIX.

Of Antiſcorbutic Water.

THE Scurvy being a Diſeaſe very common in *England*, this Antiſcorbutic Water will be of great uſe.

Recipe for making ten Gallons of Antiſcorbutic Water.

Take of the Leaves of Water-creſſes, Garden and Sea Scurvy-graſs, and Brooklime of each twenty Handfuls; of Pinetops, Germander, Horehound, and the leſſer Centory, of each ſixteen Handfuls; of the Roots of Briony and ſharp-pointed Dock, of each ſix Pounds; of Muſtard-ſeed one Pound and a Half. Digeſt the whole in ten Gallons of Proof Spirit, and two Gallons of Water, and draw of by a gentle Fire.

This is a good Water for the Purpoſes expreſſed in the Title, *viz.* againſt Scorbutic Diſorders. It is alſo good in Tremblings and Diſorders of the Nerves.

N CHAP.

CHAP. XX.

Of compound Horse-radish Water.

THERE are several Methods of making this compound Water; but the three following Recipes are the best that has hitherto appeared.

Recipe for making ten Gallons of compound Horse-radish Water.

Take of the Leaves of fresh Garden Scurvy-grass sixteen Pounds; of fresh Horse-radish Root, and the yellow Part of Seville Orange-peel of each eight Pounds; of Nutmegs two Pounds. Cut and bruise these Ingredients, and digest them twenty-four Hours in ten Gallons of Proof Spirit and two Gallons of Water; after which draw off ten Gallons with a gentle Fire.

Or,

Take of the fresh Roots of Horse-radish nine Pounds; of the Leaves of Water-cresses and of Garden Scurvy-grass, of each six Pounds; of the outward, or yellow Peel of Oranges and Lemons, of each nine Ounces; of *Winter*'s Bark twelve Ounces; of Nutmegs three Ounces. Cut, bruise and digest the Ingredients in ten Gallons of

Proof

Proof Spirit, and two Gallons of Water, and draw off ten Gallons as before.

Or,

Take of the Leaves of Garden and Sea Scurvy-graſs freſh gathered in the Spring, of each ſeven Pounds; Brook-lime, Water-creſſes, and Horſe-radiſh-root of each ten Pounds; of *Winter*'s Bark and Nutmegs of each ten Ounces; of the outer Peel of Lemons one Pound; of Arum-root freſh gathered two Pounds; Proof Spirit ten Gallons, Water two Gallons. Bruiſe and ſlice the Ingredients; digeſt the whole, and draw off ten Gallons as before.

Either of the above Receipes will produce an excellent Water, againſt all Obſtructions of the Kidnies and other Viſcera. It is alſo of great Service in the Jaundice, Cachexies and Dropſies; and in all Scorbutic Caſes, it is equal to any Medicine; as it opens the minute Paſſages, promotes Tranſpiration, and cleanſes the Skin, and other ſmall Glands, which are filled with groſs Particles to the Detriment of their proper Offices.

N 2   CHAP.

CHAP. XXI.

Of Treacle Water.

THIS Water is made in a very different Manner, by different Persons; but the following Recipes are the best for this Purpose.

Recipe for making ten Gallons of Treacle Water.

Take of the fresh and green Husks of Walnuts four Pounds and a Half; of the Roots of Butter-burr, three Pounds; of Angelica and Master-wort, of each one Pound and a Half; of Zedoary twelve Ounces; of the Leaves of Rue and Scordium of each eighteen Ounces; of Venice Treacle three Pounds; digest them together four Days in twelve Gallons of Proof Spirit, and two Gallons of Water; after which draw off ten Gallons, to which add a Gallon and a Half of distilled Vinegar.

Or,

Take of the Rind of green Walnuts five Pounds; of Rue four Pounds; of Carduus, Marigold, and Balm, of each three Pounds; of fresh gathered Butter-burr-roots two Pounds and a Half; of Burdock-root one Pound and a Half; of green Scordium twelve Handfuls; of Venice Treacle and

Mithridate

Mithridate of each two Pounds and a Half; Proof Spirit twelve Gallons; and Water two Gallons. Digeſt, and draw off ten Gallons, as before; to which add a Gallon and a Half of diſtilled Vinegar.

Some inſtead of diſtilled Vinegar unadviſedly add a proportional Quantity of Spirit of Vitriol, or other Mineral Acid, to their Treacle Water; but this Practice is very pernicious; and intirely alters the Nature of the Medicine. Vinegar is an Acid made by a double Fermentation, and therefore of a different Nature from the acid Juices of Vegetables, whether Oranges, Lemons, Citrons, Limes, Crabs, Barberies, &c, as alſo from thoſe of Minerals, whether Vitriol, Sulphur, &c. It is indeed, like them, acid on the Tongue; but then it liquifies the Blood, is antipeſtilential, ſuddenly cures Drunkenneſs, Surfeits, the Plague, and does a thouſand Things both as a Menſtruum and Medicine, which they will not. This is an admirable and ſprightly Alexipharmic and Sudorific, to which the Vinegar added, greatly contributes, and therefore good in Fevers, the Small-pox, Meaſles, and other peſtilential Diſorders.

CHAP. XXII.

Compound Camomile-flower Water.

THE Camomile-flowers generally used are the double Sort, consisting wholly of Petals or Flower Leaves, without any Appearance of Stamina or Pistil, or the other Parts of Fructification, which in the single Flowers shew themselves in the Middle in Form of yellow Threads. But tho' the double Flowers are the Sort commonly used, they are not the best, or those which ought to be chosen. The single Flowers, or those which consist of only a single Series of Leaves, or Petals, in Form of Rays, surrounding a Cluster of yellow Threads or Stamina, have much more Virtue. It is indeed in these Stamina and their Apices, that great Part of the Virtue of the Flower resides, and these are wanting in the double Flowers.

Recipe for making ten Gallons of compound Camomile-flower Water.

Take of dried Camomile-flowers, five Pounds; of the outer Peel of Oranges, ten Ounces; of the Leaves of common Wormwood, and Penny-royal, of each twenty Handfuls; of the Seeds of Anise, Cummin,

min, and sweet Fennel, the Berries of Bay and Juniper, of each five Ounces. Digest these Ingredients two Days in ten Gallons of Proof Spirit, and three Gallons of Water, and draw off ten Gallons with a gentle Fire.

This is a very good Carminative and Stomachic; good in all Cholics and other Disorders of the Bowels from Wind. It also provokes the Appetite and promotes a good Digestion. Its Virtues as a Stomachic will not be less when made from the double Flowers; but if intended as a Carminative it should be made with the single Flowers.

C H A P. XXIII.

Imperial Water.

THIS Cordial Water has its Name from the great Opinion conceived of it by its first Inventors; and tho' their Opinion was, perhaps, justly founded, yet it is not at present so much in use as formerly.

Receipe for making ten Gallons of Imperial Water.

Take of the dried Peels of Citrons and Oranges, of Nutmegs, Cloves, and Cinnamon, of each one Pound; of the Roots of

N 4 Cypress,

Cyprefs, Florintine Orrice, Calamus Aromaticus, of each eight Ounces; of Zedoary, Galangal and Ginger, of each four Ounces; of the Tops of Lavender and Rofemary, of each fixteen Handfuls; of the Leaves of Marjoram, Mint, and Thyme, of each eight Handfuls; of the Leaves of white and damafk Rofes, of each twelve Handfuls. Digeft the whole two Days in ten Gallons of Proof Spirit, and four Gallons of damafk Rofe Water; after which draw off ten Gallons.

All the Ingredients in Compofition coincide in one intention, and are fuch as will give their Virtues by Diftillation; Circumftances that cannot be faid of many other compound Waters. It is a very good Cephalic, and of great ufe in all nervous Cafes. It is alfo a very pleafant Dram, efpecially if dulcified with fine Sugar, and good upon any fudden Sicknefs of the Stomach.

C H A P. XXIV.

Of Compound Piony Water.

THE Piony, from whence this Compound Water takes its Name, is a Plant divided into Male and Female; but the former is the Sort intended to be ufed in this Compofition. The Male and Female Plants

Plants are diſtinguiſhed both by their Roots and Leaves. The Male has a ſhining blackiſh Leaf, from which the Female differs by being lighter coloured. The Root of the Male kind is more bulbous, ſhorter, and branched than that of the Female, whoſe Shoots are much longer and thinner.

Recipe for making ten Gallons of compound Piony Water.

Take of the Roots of Male Piony, twelve Ounces; of thoſe wild of Valerian, nine Ounces; and of thoſe of white Dittany ſix Ounces; of Piony-ſeed four Ounces and a Half; of the freſh Flowers of Lilly of the Valley, one Pound and a Half; of thoſe of Lavender, Arabian Stæchas, and Roſemary, of each nine Ounces; of the Tops of Betony, Marjoram, Rue and Sage, of each ſix Ounces; ſlice and bruiſe the Ingredients, and digeſt them four Days in ten Gallons of Proof Spirit and two Gallons of Water; after which draw off ten Gallons.

Or,

Take of the Flowers of Lillies of the Valley freſh gathered, and Male Piony-root, of each two Pounds; of Cinnamon and Cubebs, of each eight Ounces; of Roſemary and Lavender Flowers, of each two

Hand-

Handfuls; of damask Rose Water two Gallons. Digest these four Days in ten Gallons of Proof Spirit, and draw off ten Gallons as before.

This is an excellent Cordial, and can be exceeded by nothing in all Nervous Cases, both in Children and grown Persons.

CHAP. XXV.

Of Nutmeg Water.

THE Nutmeg is a Kernel of a large Fruit not unlike the Peach, and is separated from that and its investient Coat the Mace, before it is sent over to us ; except when the whole Fruit is sent over in Preserve, by way of Sweet-meat, or as a Curiosity. There are two Kinds of Nutmegs, the one called by Authors the Male, and the other the Female. The Female is the Kind in common use, and is of the Shape of an Olive: The Male is long and cylindric, and has less of the fine aromatic Flavour than the other, so that it is much less esteemed, and People who trade largely in Nutmegs will seldom buy it. Besides this oblong kind of Nutmeg we sometimes meet with others of very irregular Figures; but these are mere *Lusus Naturæ*, being produced by the same Tree. The long or Male Nutmeg, as we term it, is, by the *Dutch*,

called

called the wild Nutmeg. It is always diſtinguiſhable from the others as well by its want of Fragrancy as by its Shape: It is very ſubject to be worm-eaten, and is ſtrictly forbid by the *Dutch* to be packed up among the other, becauſe it will be the means of their being worm-eaten alſo by the Inſects getting from it into them, and breeding in all Parts of the Parcel. The largeſt, heavieſt, and moſt unctuous of the Nutmegs are to be choſen, ſuch as are of the Shape of an Olive, and of the moſt fragrant ſmell.

Recipe for making ten Gallons of Nutmeg Water.

Take of Nutmegs bruiſed one Pound; Proof Spirit ten Gallons; Water two Gallons. Digeſt them two Days, and then draw off ten Gallons with a briſk Fire. You may either dulcify it or not as occaſion offers.
Or,
Take of Nutmegs bruiſed one Pound; Orange-peel two Ounces; Spirit ten Gallons; Water two Gallons. Digeſt, and diſtil as before.

This is an excellent Cephalic and Cordial Water; agreeable to the Palate, comfortable to the Stomach, and grateful to the Nerves. It powerfully diſcuſſes Wind and Vapours
from

the Stomach and Bowels, and is therefore of great Service in the Cholic, and Griping of the Bowels.

CHAP. XXVI.

Of Compound Bryony Water.

THE white Bryony-root, from whence this Water takes its Name, is one of the largest Roots we are acquainted with. It is of an oblong Shape, and is frequently met with of the Thickneſs of a Man's Arm, ſometimes of twice or three times that Bigneſs. Its Texture is ſomewhat lax and ſpungy; conſiderably heavy, but ſo ſoft that the thickeſt Pieces are eaſily cut through with one Stroke of a Knife: It is very juicy, and is externally of a browniſh or yellowiſh white Colour, and of a pure white within: It is of a diſagreeable Smell, and an acrid and nauſeous Taſte.

Recipe for ten Gallons of Compound Bryony Water.

Take of the Roots of Bryony four Pounds; wild Valerian-root one Pound; of Pennyroyal and Rue, of each two Pounds; of the Flowers of Fever-few, and Tops of Savin, of each four Ounces; of the Rind of freſh Orange-peel, and Lovage-ſeeds,

of

of each Half a Pound: Cut or bruife thefe
Ingredients and infufe them in eleven Gallons of Proof Spirit, and two Gallons of
Water, and draw off ten Gallons with a
gentle Heat.

Or,

Take of frefh Bryony-root four Pounds;
of the Leaves of Rue and Mugwort, of
each four Pounds; of the Tops of Savin
fix Handfuls; of Fever-few, Catmint and
Pennyroyal, of each four Handfuls; of
Orange-peel eight Ounces; of Myrrh
four Ounces; of *Ruffia* Caftor, two Ounces;
Proof Spirit eleven Gallons, Water two Gallons. Digeft, and diftil as before.

This Compofition is very unpalatable, but
excellently adapted to the Intention of an
Hyfteric, in which Cafes it is ufed with
Succefs. It is very forcing upon the Ute-
rus, and therefore given to promote Deli-
very, and forward the proper Cleanfings afterwards; as alfo to open Menftrual Ob-
ftructions, and in abundance of other Female Complaints. It is alfo good againft
Convulfions in Children, and of fervice in all
nervous Complaints in either Sex.

It may not be amifs to obferve here, that
the oily Parts of the Ingredients will often
render the Water foul and milky. If
therefore the Diftiller defires to have it fine
and

and tranfparent, the Receiver muft be removed as foon as the Liquor at the Worm appears the leaft turbid, which will be long before the Faints begin to rife. The Water, however, is not the worfe for being milky, with regard to its Medicinal Virtue. Some, when the Liquor is milky, throw in a little burnt Allum to fine it; but this fhould never be done, becaufe it fpoils the Medicine.

CHAP. XXVII.

Of compound Baum Water, commonly called
Eau de Carmes.

THIS has its Name (*Eau de Carmes*) from the Carmelite Friars who were the Inventors of it. The great Profit accruing to thefe Fathers, from the Sale of this Cordial, induced them to keep the Method of making it a Secret; but notwithftanding all their Care the Secret has at laft been difcovered, and the following is the Method by which they prepare it.

Recipe for two Gallons of Eau de Carmes.

Take of the frefh Leaves of Baum four Pounds; of the yellow Peel, or Rind of Lemons, two Pounds; of Nutmegs and Coriander-feeds of each one Pound; of
Cloves,

Cloves, Cinnamon, and Angelica-root, of each Half a Pound. Pound the Leaves, bruise the other Ingredients, and put them with two Gallons of fine Proof Spirit into a large Glass Alembic (the Figure of which with its Head is represented on the Plate, Fig. 7.) stop the Mouth, and place it in a Bath-Heat to digest two or three Days. Then open the Mouth of the Alembic, and add a Gallon of Baum Water, and shake the whole well together. After this place the Alembic in Balneum Mariæ, and distil till the Ingredients are almost dry; and preserve the Water thus obtained in Bottles well stopped.

This Water has been long famous both at *London* and *Paris*, and carried thence to most Parts of *Europe*. It is a very elegant Cordial, and very extraordinary Virtues are attributed to it; for it is esteemed very efficacious not only in Lowness of Spirits, but even in Apoplexies; and is greatly commended in Cases of the Gout in the Stomach.

CHAP.

CHAP. XXVIII.

Of Ladies Water.

THIS Water has its Name from its Dear-ness, being much fitter for the Closet than to be sold in a Shop; but as it is an excellent Cordial, I could not omit giving it a Place here.

Recipe for one Quart of Ladies Water.

Take of Sugar-candy one Pound; of Canary Wine six Ounces, Rose Water four Ounces; boil them into a Syrup, and mix with it of Heavenly Water (described Chap. xxx.) one Quart; of Ambergrise and Musk of each eighteen Grains; of Saffron fifteen Grains; yellow Saunders two Drams. Di-gest the whole three Days in a Vessel close stoped, and decant the clear for use.

This is an extraordinary Cordial where the Perfumes are not offensive. It is too rich to be drank alone, and therefore should be mixed with Water, or some other Liquid.

CHAP.

CHAP. XVII.

Of Cephalic Water.

THIS Water has its Name from its ufe, being one of the beft Cephalic Waters known.

Recipe for ten Gallons of Cephalic Water.

Take of Male Piony-root twelve Ounces; of Angelica and Valerian of each four Ounces and a Half; of the Leaves of Rofemary, Marjoram and Baum; of the Flowers of Lavender, Betony, Piony, Marigolds, Sage, Rofemary, Lilies of the Valley, and of the Lime Tree, of each three Handfuls; of Stæchus, or *French* Lavender, four Ounces and a Half; of red Rofes and Cowflips, of each fix Handfuls; of Rhodium Wood and yellow Saunders, of each two Ounces and a Half; of Nutmegs four Ounces and a Half; of Galangals, an Ounce and a Half; of Cardamoms and Cubebs, of each one Ounce. Bruife thefe Ingredients, and digeft them ten Days in eleven Gallons of Proof Spirit, and two Gallons of Water, after which add three Pounds of Cinnamon, and digeft two Days more; and then draw off ten Gallons with a pretty brifk

O Fire

Fire, and dulcify it to your Palate with fine Sugar.

This is an excellent Cordial, of great Use in Faintings or Sinking of the Spirits, and to remove any sudden Nauseas or Sickness at the Stomach.

CHAP. XXX.

Of Heavenly Water; or, Aqua Cælestis.

THIS Water has its Name from the great opinion its Inventors had of it; but at present it is not so much called for as formerly.

Recipe for ten Gallons of Heavenly Water.

Take of Cinnamon, Mace, and Cubebs, of each three Ounces; Ginger one Ounce and a Half; Cloves, Galangal, Nutmegs, and Cardamoms, of each one Ounce; Zedoary one Ounce and a Half; Fennel-seeds one Ounce; of the Seeds of Anise, wild Carrot and Basil, of each Half an Ounce; Roots of Angelica, Valerian, Calamus Aromaticus, Leaves of Thyme, Calamint, Penniroyal, Mint, Mother of Thyme, and Marjoram, of each an Ounce; Flowers of red Roses, Sage, Rosemary, and Stæchas, of each six Drams; Citron-peel an Ounce: bruise all these Ingredients and digest them three Days in eleven Gallons of Proof Spirit, and four Gallons of Water; after which draw off ten Gallons, lions, with a pretty brisk Fire; and dulcify the Goods with fine Sugar, adding Ambergrise and Musk of each three Scruples.

The Perfumes ordered to be added with the Sugar, rendering the Medicine offensive to some People, they may be omitted at pleasure. It is esteemed very efficacious in all nervous Complaints, particularly Palsies, Loss of Memory, and the like. In all Decays of Age, and languishing Constitutions, it is exceeded by nothing in suddenly raising the Spirits, and warming the Blood.

CHAP. XXXI.

Of Spirituous Penniroyal Water.

THE Plant from whence this Water has its Name has been already described Chap. xiii. Part II.

Recipe for ten Gallons of Spirituous Penniroyal Water.

Take of the Leaves of Penniroyal dried fifteen Pounds; Proof Spirit ten Gallons; Water two Gallons: draw off ten Gallons with a gentle Fire.

This is a good Carminative, of use in Cholics and Gripings of the Bowels; also in Plurisies and the Jaundice: It is of known

Efficacy

Efficacy in promoting the Menſes and other Diſorders of the Female Sex.

CHAP. XXXII.

Of Compound Parſley Water.

THIS Plant from whence the Water is denominated is the common Parſley of our Gardens, an Herb too well known to need Deſcription.

Recipe for ten Gallons of compound Parſley Water.

Take of Parſley-root, one Pound and a Quarter; freſh Horſe-radiſh Root, and Juniper-berries, of each fifteen Ounces; the Tops of St. John's-wort, biting Arſmart, and Elder-flowers, of each ten Ounces; the Seeds of wild Carrot, ſweet Fennel, and Parſley, of each ſeven Ounces and a Half; ſlice and bruiſe the Ingredients, and digeſt them four Days in eleven Gallons of Spirit, and two Gallons of Water; after which draw off ten Gallons.

This is a very good Diuretic, frees the Kidnies from Sand and other Matter, which often forms Gravel and Stones. It is alſo good in cholic Pains ariſing from a Stone in the

the Bladder, and drains off all ill Humours by Urine.

C H A P. XXXIII.

Of Carminative Water.

THIS Water has its Name from its uſe, being an excellent Carminative.

Recipe for ten Gallons of Carminative Water.

Take of freſh Camomile-flowers, four Pounds; Dill-ſeed two Pounds and a Half; Leaves of Baum, Origany, and Thyme, of each one Pound; Seeds of Aniſe and Fennel of each ſix Ounces; Cummin-ſeed four Ounces; Peels of Oranges and Citrons, of each eight Ounces; Juniper and Bayberries, of each ſix Ounces; Cinnamon eight Ounces; Mace four Ounces. Digeſt theſe Ingredients, bruiſed in eleven Gallons of Proof Spirit, and two Gallons of Water; after which draw of ten Gallons; and dulcify it with fine Sugar.

This is an admirable Carminative, and therefore good in all Cholicky Pains and Gripings of the Bowels; and to remove Sickneſs and Nauſeas from the Stomach.

CHAP. XXXIV.

Of Gout Water.

THIS Water alſo has its Name from its uſe, being of great Service in that Diſtemper.

Recipe for ten Gallons of Gout Water.

Take of the Flowers of Camomile, Leaves of Penniroyal, Lavender, Marjoram, Roſemary, Sage, and Ground-pine, of each eight Ounces; Myrrh four Ounces; Cloves and Cinnamon of each one Ounce; Roots of Piony two Ounces; Pellitory of *Spain*, and Cypreſs Orrice, of each one Ounce; the leſſer Cardamoms and Cubebs, of each Half an Ounce; Nutmegs, two Ounces: Cut and bruiſe theſe Ingredients and digeſt them four Days in eleven Gallons of Proof Spirit and two Gallons of Water; then draw off ten Gallons, and dulcify with fine Sugar,

This is a very good Water in all nervous Caſes; and a continued moderate Uſe of it will comfort and fortify the Fibres, ſo as to prevent the Diſcharge of ſuch Juices upon the Joints as cauſe arthritic Pains and Swellings. It is alſo of excellent Uſe in Palſies, Epilepſies, and Loſs of Memory; particularly when theſe Diſtempers proceed

from

from old Age, or when the principal Springs of Life begin to decay.

CHAP. XXXV.

Of Anhalt Water.

THIS Water is fuppofed to have been invented by a celebrated Phyfician of *Anhalt*, a Province of the Circle of Upper *Saxony*.

Recipe for making ten Gallons of Anhalt Water.

Take of the beft Turpentine a Pound and a Half; Olibanum three Ounces; Aloes-wood powdered one Ounce; Grains of Maftick, Cloves, July-flowers, or Rofemary-flowers, Nutmegs and Cinnamon of each two Ounces and a Half; Saffron one Ounce; powder the whole and digeft them fix Days in eleven Gallons of Spirit of Wine; adding two Scruples of Mufk tied up in a Rag; and draw off in Balneum Mariæ till it begins to run foul.

This Water is a high aromatic Cordial, invigorates the Inteftines, and thereby promotes Digeftion and difpels Flatulencies. It is alfo in great Repute as a fovereign Remedy for Catarrhs and Pains arifing from

O 4 Colds;

Colds; as also in Palsies, Epilepsies, Apoplexies and Lethargies, the Parts affected being well rubbed with it.

C H A P. XXXVI.

Of Vulnerary Water, or, *Eau d'Arquebusade*.

THIS Vulnerary Water is greatly esteemed abroad; and if properly tried, there is no doubt of its obtaining the same Reputation here.

Recipe for five Gallons of Vulnerary Water.

Take of the Leaves, Flowers and Roots of Comfrey, Leaves of Mugwort, Sage, and Bugle, of each eight Handfuls; Leaves of Betony, Sanicle, or Ox-eye Daisy, the greater Figwort, Plantain, Agrimony, Vervain, Wormwood, and Fennel, of each four Handfuls; St. John's-wort, Birth-wort, Orpine, Paul's-betony, the lessor Centory, Yarrow, Tobacco, Mouse-ear, Mint, and Hyssop, of each two Handfuls: Cut them, bruise them well in a Mortar, and pour on them three Gallons of white Wine and two Gallons and a Half of Proof Spirit; digest the whole six Days with a gentle Heat, in a Vessel close stopped: after which distil off with gentle Fire, about five Gallons,

lons, or till it begins to run milky from the Worm.

This Water is of excellent Service in Contufions, Tumors attending Difloca-tions, Fractures and Mortifications, the Part affected being bathed with it. Some alfo ufe it to deterge foul Ulcers, and incarn Wounds; from whence it was called Vul-nerary Water.

CHAP. XXXVII.

Of Cedrat Water.

THE Fruit called *Cedrat* by the *French* is a Species of the Citron, called by Botanifts *Citratum Florentinum, fruÅtu Mucronato & recurvo, Cortice verrucofo Odo-ratiffimo*, Florentine Citron, with a pointed Fruit, which is recurved, and a warted fweet fmelling Rind. This Fruit is in fo great Efteem, that they have been fold at *Florence* for two Shillings each, and are often fent as Prefents to the Courts of Princes. It is only found in Perfection, in the Plain between *Pifa* and *Legborn*; and tho' the Trees which produce this Fruit have been tranfplanted into other Parts of *Italy*, yet they are found to lofe much of that excellent Tafte with which they abound in thofe Parts.

Recipe

Recipe for a Gallon of Cedrat Water.

Take the yellow Rinds of five Cedrats, a Gallon of fine Proof Spirit, and two Quarts of Water: Digeſt the whole twenty-four Hours in a Veſſel cloſe ſtoped; after which draw off one Gallon in Balneum Mariæ, and dulcify with fine Loaf Sugar.

This is eſteemed the fineſt Cordial yet known; but as it is very difficult to procure the Fruit here, I ſhall give the Method of making this celebrated Cordial, with the Eſſence or eſſential Oil of the Cedrat, which is often imported from *Italy*.

Recipe for a Gallon of Cedrat Water with the Eſſence of the Fruit.

Take of the fineſt Loaf Sugar reduced to Powder a Quarter of a Pound, put into it a Glaſs Mortar, with one Hundred and twenty Drops of the Eſſence of Cedrat, rub them together with a Glaſs Peſtle, put them into a Glaſs Alembic with a Gallon of fine Proof Spirits and a Quart of Water. Place the Alembic in Balneum Mariæ, and draw off one Gallon, or till the Faints begin to riſe; and dulcify with fine Sugar.

You

You may make this Water without Diftillation, by mixing the Effence with the
Sugar, as before directed, and diffolving it
in the Spirit and Water directed as above.
But the Water will be foul and milky, and
therefore you muft filtrate it thro' Paper,
which will reftore its Brightnefs and Tran-
fparency.

But whatever Method is ufed, you muft be
very careful that the Spirit been tirely freed
from its effential Oil ; and therefore if your
Spirit be not very cleanly rectified, it will be
advifeable to ufe *French* Brandy, left the fine
Flavour fo highly efteemed in this Cordial
be deftroyed by the Spirit.

C H A P. XXXVIII.

Of Bergamot Water.

THE Bergamot is a Species of the Citron, produced at firft cafually by an
Italian's Grafting a Citron on the Stock of
a Burgamot Pear Tree, whence the Fruit
produced by this Union participated both of
the Citron Tree and Pear Tree. The Inventor is faid to have kept the Difcovery a
a long Time a Secret, and enriched himfelf
by it.

The

The Bergamot is a very fine Fruit both in Tafte and Smell; and its Effence or effential Oil highly efteemed.

Recipe for a Gallon of Bergamot Water.

Take the outer Rind of three Bergamots, a Gallon of Proof Spirit, and two Quarts of Water. Draw off one Gallon in Balneum Mariæ, and dulcify with fine Sugar.

If you make your Bergamot Water from the Effence or effential Oil, obferve the fame Directions as given in the preceeding Chapter for making Cedrat Water. One Hundred and fixty Drops of the Effence will be fufficient for a Gallon of Spirit, and fo in Proportion for a greater or fmaller Quantity.

CHAP. XXXIX.

Of Orange Cordial Water; or, Eau de Bigarade.

THE Orange called by the *French* Bigarade, is called by Botanifts *Aurantium maximum, verrucofo Cortice*, the large worted Orange.

It

It is a large and beautiful Fruit, and greatly efteemed for the Fragrancy of its Effence. It is common in diverfe Parts of *Italy*, *Spain*, and *Provence* in *France*.

Recipe for making a Gallon of Orange Cordial.

Take of the outer or yellow Part of the Rinds of fourteen Bigarades; Half an Ounce of Nutmegs; a Quarter of an Ounce of Mace, a Gallon of fine Proof Spirit, and two Quarts of Water. Digeft all thefe together two Days in a clofe Veffel; after which draw off a Gallon with a gentle Fire, and dulcify with fine Sugar.

This Cordial is greatly efteemed abroad, and would be the fame here if fufficiently known.

If the Orange Peels are not eafily procured, one Hundred and forty Drops of the Effence may be ufed in their ftead, and the Water will be nearly equal to that made from the Peels.

CHAP.

C H A P. XL.

Of Jasmine Water.

THERE are several Species of Jasmine, but that Sort intended here is what the Gardeners call, *Spanish* White or *Catalonian* Jasmine. This is one of the most Beautiful of all the Species of Jasmine; the Flowers much larger than any of the others, of a red Colour on the Outside, and extremely fragrant. But if the Flowers of this Species cannot be procured, those of the common Sort may be used, but the Quantity must be considerably augmented.

Recipe for a Gallon of Jasmine Water.

Take of *Spanish* Jasmine-flowers twelve Ounces; Essence of Florentine Citron, or Burgamot, eight Drops; fine Proof Spirit a Gallon, Water two Quarts. Digest two Days in a close Vessel, after which draw off one Gallon, and dulcify with fine Loaf Sugar.

This is a most excellent Cordial, and deserves to be more known here than it is at present.

CHAP.

C H A P. XLI.

Of the Cordial Water of Montpelier.

THIS Water has its Name from the Place where it was firft made, and what is now brought from thence is ftill in great Reputation.

Recipe for a Gallon of the Cordial Water of Montpelier.

Take of the yellow Rinds of two Berga-mots, or fifty Drops of the Effence of that Fruit; Cloves and Mace of each Half an Ounce; Proof Spirit a Gallon; Water one Quart: Digeft two Days in a clofe Veffel, draw off a Gallon, and dulcify with fine Sugar.

C H A P. XLII.

Of Father Andrew's *Water.*

THIS Water has its Name from its In-ventor; and is greatly efteemed in France.

Recipe

Recipe for a Gallon of Father Andrew's Water.

Take of white Lilly-flowers eight Handfuls; Orange-flowers four Ounces; Rose Water a Quart; Proof Spirit a Gallon; Water a Quart: Draw off a Gallon in Balneum Mariæ, and dulcify with fine Sugar.

C H A P. XLIII.

Of the Water of Father Barnabas.

THIS Water has also its Name from its Inventor, a Jesuit of *Paris*.

Recipe for a Gallon of the Water of Father Barnabas.

Take of the Roots of Angelica four Ounces; of Cinnamon and Orris-root, of each Half an Ounce; bruise these Ingredients in a Mortar; put them into an Alembic, with a Gallon of Proof Spirit and two Quarts of Water; draw off a Gallon with a pretty brisk Fire.

C H A P.

C H A P. XLIV.

Of the Water of the four Fruits.

THIS Water has its Name from the four Fruits in its Compoſition, namely the Cedrat or Florentine Citron, the Bergamot, the common Citron, and the *Portugal* Orange.

Recipe for a Gallon of the Water of the four Fruits.

Take of the Eſſence of Cedrat, fifty Drops; of the Eſſence of Bergamot thirty-ſix Drops; of the Eſſence of Citron ſixty Drops; and of the Eſſence of *Portugal* Orange ſixty-four Drops; fine Proof Spirit one Gallon; Water two Quarts; draw off with a pretty briſk Fire till the Faints begin to riſe, and dulcify with fine Sugar.

This is a very pleaſant and odoriferous Cordial, and in great Eſteem in *France.*

P   CHAP.

CHAP. XLV.

Of the Water of the four Spices.

THIS Water alfo derives it Name from the four Spices from whence it is drawn, *viz.* Cloves, Mace, Nutmegs, and Cinnamon.

Recipe for a Gallon of the Water of the four Spices.

Take of Cinnamon two Ounces; Nutmegs and Cloves, of each three Drams; Mace fix Drams; bruife the Spices in a Mortar, and add Proof Spirit a Gallon, and Water two Quarts. Digeft twenty-four Hours in a clofe Veffel, and diftil with a brifk Fire till the Faints begin to rife; and dulcify with fine Sugar.

This is an excellent Stomachic, good in all Depreffions of the Spirits and paralytic Diforders.

CHAP.

CHAP. XLVI.

Of the Water of the four Seeds.

THIS Water has its Name from the four Seeds from whence is it drawn, *viz.* the Seeds of fweet Fennel, Coriander, Angelica, and Anife.

Recipe for ten Gallons of the Water of the four Seeds.

Take of fweet Fennel-feed feven Ounces; Coriander-feed nine Ounces; of the Seeds of Angelica and Anife, of each three Ounces; bruife all thefe in a Mortar, and put them into the Still with ten Gallons and a Half of Proof Spirits, and two Gallons of Water; draw off with a gentle Fire till the Faints begin to rife, and dulcify with fine Sugar.

This Water is a very good Carminative, good in Cholics, Naufeas of the Stomach, and Gripings of the Bowels.

CHAP.

CHAP. XLVII.

Of the Divine Water.

THIS is one of those Waters whose Names have rendered them famous. The Basis of this Water is Orange-flowers, the other Ingredients being added to diversify the Flavour, and render it more agreeable.

Recipe for a Gallon of Divine Water.

Take of Orange-flowers fresh gathered two Pounds; Coriander-seed three Ounces; Nutmegs Half an Ounce; bruise the Nutmegs and Coriander-seeds; and put them, together with the Orange-flowers, into an Alembic with a Gallon of Proof Spirit and two Quarts of Water; draw off the Liquor with a gentle Fire, till the Faints begin to rise, and dulcify with fine Sugar.

This is a very pleasant Cordial, both with regard to its Smell and Taste; and on that Account in great Esteem abroad.

CHAP.

CHAP. XLVIII.

Of Roman Water.

THIS Water has its Name from its being made firft at *Rome* ; and from
whence great Quantities are ftill exported
to different Parts of *Europe.*

Recipe for a Gallon of Roman Water.

Take the outer or yellow Peels of fix
Citrons; two Drams of Mace bruifed; a
Gallon of Proof Spirit, and two Quarts of
Water: Draw off with a gentle Fire till
the Faints begin to rife, and dulcify with
fine Sugar.

This Water is generally of a red or purple Colour, the former of which may be
eafily given by infufing in it a few Grains
of Cochineal, or the red Parts of Clove
Gilly-flowers; and the latter by adding to
the above a few Violets. When the Colour
is extracted, run the Liquor through the
filtrating Bag, and it will be very bright
and clear.

C H A P. XLIX.

Of Barbadoes *Water.*

THERE is a great Variety of Waters called by this Name, made by foreign Diftillers; but the following Recipes will be fufficient to fhew the Diftiller the Method of making them, and how to vary the Flavour of his Waters, fo as to adapt them to the Tafte of his Cuftomers.

Recipe for a Gallon of rectified Barbadoes *Water.*

Take the outer Rind of eight large Florentine Citrons; Half an Ounce of Cinnamon bruifed, and a Gallon of rectified Spirit. Diftil to a Drynefs in Balneum Mariæ. Then diffolve two Pounds of Sugar in a Quart of Water, and mix it with the diftilled Liquor, and run it thro' the filtrating Bag, which will render it bright and fine.

Recipe for making a Gallon of amber-coloured Barbadoes *Water.*

Take of the yellow Rinds of fix Bergamots, Half an Ounce of Cinnamon, and two Drams of Cloves. Bruife the Spices and digeft the whole fix Days in a Gallon

of

of rectified Spirit; and then add a Dram of Saffron, and let the whole ſtand ſix Days longer in Digeſtion; diſſolve two Pounds of fine Sugar in a Quart of Water, add it to the Tincture, and run it thro' the filtrating Bag.

After the ſame manner may be made *Barbadoes* Waters of different Kinds, by adding Lemon, or Orange-peels inſtead of thoſe of Citron or Bergamot; or, by varying the Spices.

C H A P. L.

Of Ros Solis.

THE Ros Solis or Sun-dew, from whence this Cordial Water has its Name, is a ſmall low Plant, with a fibrous Root, from whence ſpring ſmall round hollowiſh Leaves, on Foot ſtalks about an Inch long, covered and fringed with ſhort red Hairs, which give a red Caſt to the whole Leaf. It grows in champaign and moſſy Grounds, in a pale red Moſs, and flowers in *May*.

Recipe for ten Gallons of Ros Solis.

Take of Ros Solis picked clean, four Pounds; Cinnamon, Cloves, and Nutmegs, of each three Ounces and a Half; Mari-

gold-

gold-flowers one Pound ; Caraway-seeds ten Ounces : Proof Spirit ten Gallons, and of Water three Gallons. Diftil with a pretty brifk Fire, till the Faints begin to rife. Then take of Liquorice Root fliced Half a Pound ; Raifins ftoned two Pounds ; red Saunders Half a Pound ; digeft thefe three Days in two Quarts of Water, and ftrain out the clear Liquor, in which diffolve three Pounds of fine Sugar, and mix it with the Spirit drawn by Diftillation.

Recipe for making ten Gallons of Ros Solis by Digeftion.

Take Ros Solis clean picked three Pounds ; Nutmegs, Mace, Cloves, and Cinnamon, the Seeds of Caraway and Coriander of each three Ounces ; Ginger, the leffer Cardamom, Zedoary, and Calamus Aromaticus, of each one Ounce ; Cubebs and yellow Saunders of each Half and Ounce ; red Saunders three Ounces ; red Rofe Leaves dried three Handfuls ; Proof Spirit ten Gallons ; digeft the whole fix Days in a Veffel clofe ftoped, and then ftrain off the clear Liquor, and dulcify it with fine Sugar.

Or,

Take Ros Solis picked three Pounds ; Cinnamon and Nutmegs, Caraway and Coriander-feeds, of each three Ounces ; Cloves, Mace,

Mace, and Ginger, of each one Ounce and a Quarter; Cubebs, Cardamoms, Zedoary, and Calamus Aromaticus, of each Half an Ounce; red Rofes dried three Ounces; Liquorice Root fliced, fix Ounces; Raifins ftoned one Pound and a Half; Cochineal and Saffron, of each three Drams; digeft the whole eight Days in ten Gallons of Proof Spirits; ftrain off, and dulcify as before.

Recipe for ten Gallons of Turin *Ros Solis.*

Take of damafk Rofes, Orange-flowers, Lilies of the Valley, and Jafmine-flowers, of each two Pounds and a Half; Cinnamon five Ounces; Cloves three Drams: Put thefe Ingredients into an Alembic, with four Gallons and a Half of Water, and draw off three Gallons, with a moderate Fire; to this Water add feven Gallons of Proof Spirit, in which a Dram of Cochineal and two Drams of Saffron has been infufed; dulcify with fine Sugar, and run the whole through the filtrating Bag.

All thefe different Kinds of Ros Solis are excellent Cordials, good in all Depreffions of the Spirits, Naufeas, and paralytic Diforders.

CHAP.

CHAP. LI.

Of Usquebaugh.

USQUEBAUGH is a very celebrated Cordial, the Basis of which is Saffron. There are different Ways of making this famous Compound; but the following are equal to any I have seen..

Recipe for ten Gallons of common Usquebaugh.

Take of Nutmegs, Cloves, and Cinnamon, of each two Ounces; of the Seeds of Anise, Caraway and Coriander, of each four Ounces; Liquorice Root sliced Half a Pound; bruise the Seeds and Spices, and put them together with the Liquorice into the Still with eleven Gallons of Proof Spirits, and two Gallons of Water; distil with a pretty brisk Fire till the Faints begin to rise. But as soon as your Still begins to work, fasten to the Nose of the Worm two Ounces of *English* Saffron tied up in a Cloth, that the Liquor may run thro' it, and extract all its Tincture, and in order to this you should often press the Saffron with your Fingers. When the Operation is finished, dulcify your Goods with fine Sugar.

Recipe

Recipe for making ten Gallons of Royal Uſquebaugh.

Take of Cinnamon, Ginger, and Corian-der-ſeed, of each three Ounces; Nutmegs four Ounces and a Half; Mace, Cloves and Cubebs, of each one Ounce and a Half. Bruiſe theſe Ingredients, and put them into an Alembic with eleven Gallons of Proof Spirit, and two Gallons of Water; and dif-til till the Faints begin to riſe; faſtening four Ounces and a Half of *Engliſh* Saffron tied in a Cloth to the End of the Worm, as directed in the preceding Recipe. Take Raiſins ſtoned four Pounds and a Half; Dates three Pounds, Liquorice Root ſliced two Pounds; digeſt theſe twelve Hours in two Gallons of Water; ſtrain out the clear Liquor, add it to that obtained by Diſtilla-tion, and dulcify the whole with fine Su-gar.

Recipe for ten Gallons of Uſquebaugh by Digeſtion.

Take of Raiſins ſtoned five Pounds; Figs ſliced one Pound and a Half; Cinnamon Half a Pound; Nutmegs three Ounces; Cloves and Mace, of each one Ounce and a Half; Liquorice two Pounds; Saffron four Ounces; bruiſe the Spices, ſlice the Li-quorice,

quorice, and pull the Saffron in pieces; digeſt theſe Ingredients eight Days in ten Gallons of Proof Spirit, in a Veſſel cloſe ſtoped; then filter the Liquor, and add to it two Gallons of *Canary* Wine, and Half an Ounce of the Tincture of Ambergreaſe.

Recipe for making ten Gallons of French Uſquebaugh.

Take of Saffron three Ounces, of the eſſential Oil or Eſſence of Florentine Citron, Bergamot, *Portugal* Orange, and Lemon, of each a Hundred Drops; Angelica-ſeed, Vanellos and Mace, of each one Ounce and a Half; Cloves and Coriander-ſeed of each three Quarters of an Ounce; bruiſe the Seeds and Spices, and put all into an Alembic with eleven Gallons of Proof Spirit, and two Gallons of Water; and draw off with a gentle Fire till the Faints begin to riſe, faſtening to the Noſe of the Worm four Ounces of Saffron in a Cloth. When the Operation is finiſhed dulcify the Goods with fine Sugar.

Theſe Waters are excellent Cephalic Cordials, and Alexipharmics; and are excelled by nothing in ſuddenly reviving the Spirits when depreſſed by Sickneſs, &c.

CHAP.

CHAP. LII.

Of Ratafia.

RATAFIA is a Liquor in great Eſteem, and moſt Perſons are acquainted with it; tho' the true Method of making it is known only to a few. There are various Kinds of Ratafia made from different Fruits. I ſhall give Recipes for making thoſe which are at preſent in moſt Eſteem; which may ſerve as Inſtances for making theſe Goods from any other Kinds of Fruit.

1. *Of red Ratafia.*

There are three Sorts of Ratafia drawn from red Fruits, diſtinguiſhed by the Epithets *fine*, *dry*, and *common*.

The Fruits moſt proper to make the red Ratafia are the black Heart Cherry, the common red Cherry, the black Cherry, the Merry or Honey Cherry, the Strawberry, the Raſberry, the red Gooſeberry, and the Mulberry.

Theſe Fruits ſhould be gathered in the Height of their reſpective Seaſons, and the largeſt and moſt beautiful of them choſen for the purpoſe.

Thus

Thus with regard to the Heart Cherry, it should be large, fleshy, and thorough but not over ripe; for then a Part of its Juice will be evaporated on the Tree: Care must be also taken, that its Colour be not decayed; but clear and almost transparent, and well tasted.

The black Cherry, or as it is often called, the black Arvon, must be extremly ripe, because it is used to colour the Ratafia when that of the other fails. The Criterion of judging when it is thoroughly ripe is its Blackness; for, when in Perfection, it is perfectly black. It should also be remembered that this Fruit is better and more profitable in Proportion to its Sweetness; as the Flavour of the Ratafia will be rendered more agreeable, and a less Quantity of Sugar necessary.

As the Gooseberry is an acid Fruit, it must be chosen as ripe as possible. The Fruit large, and the Skin and Husk so transparent as to see the Seeds through it. The Gooseberry should be used immediately after its being gathered; for it is very liable to ferment, which will inevitably spoil the Ratafia. Gooseberries are chiefly used to render the Ratafia dry or sharp, and consequently less soft; and therefore their Quantity should always be proportioned to that Intention. The

The Merry to be good fhould be fmall, black, the Skin tranfparent, full of Liquor of deep black Purple Colour. The greateft Care fhould be taken, that it be frefh gathered, and not rotten. It corrects the acid Juices of the other Fruits by its Sweetnefs, foftens the Compofition; and is of great Service in colouring the Ratafia.

The Mulberry is of the greateft Service in colouring the Ratafia. It fhould be chofen large, and fully ripe, at which time it is of a black Purple Colour. Its Tafte alfo greatly contributes to render the Ratafia of a pleafant and agreeable Flavour.

The Strawberry greatly contributes to increafe the rich Flavour of the Ratafia; but it muft be chofen ripe, and large; frefh gathered and not bruifed. Another Caution neceffary to this Fruit is, that they are gathered in dry warm Weather; for if gathered in rainy Weather they will want that fine Tafte, for which they are fo greatly valued.

The Rafberry is alfo added to augment the Richnefs of the Liquor, to which its elegant perfumy Tafte greatly contributes; by its agreeable Acidity it renders the Flavour more

brifk

brisk and agreeable. It must be fresh gathered, full ripe, and free from Spots and Mouldness, which this Fruit is particularly subject to.

Having thus concisely enumerated the Qualities requisite in the several Fruits, to render the Ratafia of a rich and elegant Flavour, we shall proceed to give the best Methods for making Ratafia from them.

Recipe for making red Ratafia, fine and soft.

Take of the black Heart Cherries twenty-four Pounds; black Cherries four Pounds; Rasberries and Strawberries, of each three Pounds: Pick these Fruits from their Stalks, and bruise them, in which Condition let them continue twelve Hours; press out the Juice, and, to every Pint of it add a Quarter of a Pound of Sugar. When the Sugar is dissolved run the whole through the filtrating Bag, and add to it three Quarts of clean Proof Spirits. Then take of Cinnamon four Ounces; of Mace an Ounce; and of Cloves two Drams. Bruise these Spices, put them into an Alembic with a Gallon of clean Proof Spirits and two Quarts of Water, and draw off a Gallon with a brisk Fire. Add as much of this spicy Spirit to your Ratafia as will render it agreeable

agreeable to your Palate; about one fourth is the uſual Proportion.

Ratafia made according to the above Recipe will be of a very rich Flavour, and elegant Colour. It may be rendered more or leſs of a ſpicy Flavour, by adding or diminiſhing the Quantity of Spirit diſtilled from the Spices.

Some in making Ratafia ſuffer the expreſſed Juices of their Fruits to ferment ſeveral Days; by this means the Vinoſity of the Ratafia is increaſed; but, at the ſame time, the elegant Flavour of the Fruits greatly diminiſhed. Wherefore if the Ratafia be deſired ſtronger or more vinous, it may be done by adding more Spirits to the expreſſed Juice; by which means the Flavour of the Fruits may be preſerved, as well as the Ratafia rendered ſtronger.

It is alſo a Method with ſome to tie the Spices in a Linen Rag, and ſuſpend them in the Ratafia. But if this Method be taken it will be neceſſary to augment the Quantity of Spirit firſt added to the expreſſed Juice. There is no great Difference in the two Methods of adding the Spices, except that by ſuſpending them in the Ratafia, the

Q Liqour

Liquor is generally rendered lefs bright and tranfparent.

There is alfo another Method practifed in making Ratafia, which is this : Take the Quantity of Fruit propofed, bruife it, and immediately pour the Spirit on the Pulp. After ftanding a Day or two exprefs the Juice and Spirit, filtrate it, and add the Sugar and Spices as before. But this Method requires more Spirit than the former, as it will be impoffible to prefs it all out of the Skins and other Parts of the Fruit remaining after the Juice is extracted.

2. *Of making fine and dry Ratafia from red Fruit.*

Tho' the Ratafia we have juft mentioned will doubtlefs pleafe the Palates of many People ; yet there are others who would prefer a different Sort ; it is therefore neceffary to know how to make dry as well as fweet Ratafia, if we are defirous of pleafing all Sorts of Palates.

Dry Ratafia is prepared in the fame manner as the preceding, but the Ingredients are different.

An equal Quantity of Cherries and Goofeberries are neceffary in making dry or fharp
Ratafia ;

Ratafia; becauſe the Acidity of the Gooſeberries gives the requiſite Flavour to this Sort of Liquor. But, at the ſame time, care muſt be taken that the Gooſeberries be fully ripe; for otherwiſe, tho' Gooſeberries are more acid before they are ripe than afterwards; yet that Acidity is not the Flavour deſired; it is acerb and rough, and will render the Flavour of the Ratafia diſagreeable. The ſame Obſervation holds good alſo with regard to the Cherries; they muſt be fully ripe as in making the ſoft Ratafia.

Inſtead of black Cherries uſed in the Compoſition of the preceding Ratafia, Mulberries ſhould be uſed in this: The reaſon for this Change is, that the Juice of the black Cherry is more ſweet and glutinous than that of the Mulberry, and therefore leſs fit for making dry Ratafia. But the Mulberries muſt be the ripeſt and blackeſt poſſible, in order to give the better Colour to the Liquor.

More Spirit and leſs Sugar in proportion to the Juice of the Fruit, is alſo required in this Compoſition than in the foregoing; but with regard to the Spices, the ſame Quantity is generally added to both.

Recipe

Recipe for making red Ratafia, fine and dry.

Take of Cherries and Gooseberries, of each thirty Pounds; Mulberries seven Pounds; Rasberries ten Pounds. Pick all these Fruits clean from their Stalks, &c. bruise them, and let them stand twelve Hours; but do not suffer them to ferment. Press out the Juice, and to every Pint add three Ounces of Sugar; when the Sugar is dissolved run it thro' the filtrating Bag, and to every five Pints of Liquor add four Pints of clean Proof Spirit; together with the same Proportion of Spirit drawn from the Spices in the foregoing Composition.

But it may not be amiss to observe here, that different Distillers use different Quantities of the Spirit drawn from the Spices. The best Method therefore is to imitate the Flavour most universally approved of, which may be easily done by adding a greater or less Proportion of the spiced Spirit.

3. *Of mixed Ratafia.*

By mixed Ratafia is meant the Juices of Fruits prepared, and ready to be mixed with the Spirit when called for.

Recipe

Recipe for making mixed Ratafia.

Ratafia is compoſed of Cherries and Gooſeberries ; of theſe the beſt are to be choſen, bruiſed, and in that Condition ſuffered to remain ſome Days to ferment. The Juice is then to be ſtrained off, the Quantity of Sugar and Brandy added, and the whole put into a Caſk and cloſe ſtopped. A Lee or Sediment will fall to the Bottom of the Caſk, which Sediment will be of great Uſe in preſerving the Ratafia.

The Proportion of black Cherries muſt be large in this Ratafia, becauſe the Colour, which this is greatly valued for, chiefly comes from the Juice of that Fruit.

The Sugar muſt not be put in at once, becauſe the Acidneſs of the Liquor would cauſe a conſiderable Efferveſcence, but by a little at a time.

Theſe Inſtructions being obſerved, a Ratafia of this Kind may be eaſily made : And as the Spirit is not to be mixed with it, till the Ratafia is called for, a large Quantity of it may be made at a ſmall Expence, when the Fruits are in Perfection, which cannot be done by the common Methods.

Recipe

Recipe for making mixed Ratafia.

Take of common Cherries, thoroughly ripe, four Hundred and fifty Pounds; Gooseberries, large and ripe, two Hundred and twenty five Pounds; black Cherries ripe and large, fifty Pounds.   Bruise these Fruits, and in that Condition let them continue three or four Days to ferment.   Then press out the Juice, and add one fifth Part of Spirit; that is, if you have two Hundred and fifty Pints of Juice you must add to it fifty Pints of Spirit.   When your Spirit and Juice are mixed put them into a Cask, and for every Pint add three Ounces of Sugar.   By this means your Ratafia will be always ready to mix with Spirit.

But as the Proportion of Spirit is but small, it will be necessary to taste your Ratafia at least every Month, lest it should ferment, and by that means lose both its Flavour and Colour.   As soon therefore as you perceive the least Alteration in your Ratafia, more Spirit must be added to stop the Fermentation; and by this Method it may be kept the whole Year.

If you have any Ratafia remaining at the End of the Year, you must mix it with that just made, adding a large Proportion
of

of black Cherries; becaufe the Colour in the old Ratafia will not be equal to that of the new. Or you may add to your old Ratafia a proper Quantity of the frefh Juice of black Cherries, which will reftore its Colour, and, in a great Meafure its Flavour too: So that if your Ratafia has been well preferved, it will, when mixed with frefh Juice of black Cherries, be but little inferior to the new.

4. *Of white Ratafia.*

As red Fruits are the Bafis of that called red Ratafia, fo, on the contrary, that made from the Juices of white Fruits is denominated white Ratafia.

There are various Kinds of Ratafia made from various Fruits; but I fhall only give Recipes for making three or four Sorts, which will be fufficient for all the reft, as the Method is nearly the fame in all.

Recipe for making Ratafia from the Mufcat, or white Frontiniac Grape.

The Berries of this Kind of Grape are large, and grow extremely clofe upon the Bunches, which are very long, and have commonly two Shoulders: The Fruit, when ripe, has a rich mufky Flavour;

Q 4

but

but it is commonly very late in Autumn, before thefe Grapes are in Perfection; and the Berries being fo very clofe upon the Bunches, detain the Moifture in the Centre; fo that they often perifh: To prevent which fome curious Perfons look over their Vines, foon after the Grapes are formed, and, with a Pair of Sciffars, cut out all fmall ones, fo as to leave the others at a moderate Diftance, whereby the Sun and Air are eafily admitted, which diffipates the Moifture, and prevents their perifhing. There is another Kind of this Grape, called by fome the white Frontiniac of *Alexandria*, and by others the *Jerufalem* Mufcat, which is a very large Grape, and, when ripe, an excellent Fruit; but is rarely brought to Perfection in *England*. The Berries of the *Jerufalem* Mufcat, are of an oval Shape, and very large. They grow very loofe on the Bunches, are very flefhy and firm, and, when ripe, are of greenifh white, and a delicate Flavour.

Either of thefe Kinds of Grapes will make very fine Ratafia; but which ever of them are chofen, they muft be picked from the Stalks, and only the fineft Berries made ufe of. The Stones muft alfo be picked out; for if they are bruifed with the Berries, the fine Flavour of the Juice will be greatly diminifhed.

When

When you have picked the Grapes from the Stalks, and taken out the Stones, prefs out the Juice, and filtrate it through a Flannel Bag. Then add the Quantity of Sugar and Spirit, and flavour it to your mind with a Spirit diftilled from Spices, in the manner explained below.

The general Proportion of Sugar and Spirit, is, to twenty Pints of the Juice, five Pounds and a Half of Sugar, ten Pints of Spirit, and what Quantity you pleafe of the fpicy Spirit.

To make the fpicy Spirit, take of Mace one Pound, Nutmegs four Ounces, Spirit three Gallons, and draw off the whole in Balneum Mariæ.

By the fame Method you may make red Ratafia from the red Frontiniac; except that the Grapes, when bruifed, muft be fuffered to ferment three or four Days, before the Juice is preffed out; becaufe the Colour, which refides principally in the Skins of the Grapes, will, by that means, be extracted.

The Berries of the red Mufcat, or red Frontiniac, are about the Size of thofe of the white; but grow much thinner on the Bunches. This Grape, when thoroughly ripe,

ripe, has the richeſt and higheſt Flavour
of any yet known ; but it muſt have a dry
Soil and a South Aſpect, otherwiſe it ſeldom
ripens well in *England*.   Beſides the above
Grape, there is another called by ſome red
Muſcat of *Alexandria*, and by others red
Jeruſalem Muſcat.   This is not quite ſo
late in ripening as the white Muſcat of
Alexandria above deſcribed ; and for that
reaſon more eſteemed.   The Berries of this
Kind are not quite ſo large as thoſe of the
white, but of the ſame Form, and equal in
Goodneſs.

5. *Of Ratiſia from Peaches.*

The Ratafia made from the Peach is the
fineſt and richeſt Flavour of any made from
ſtoned Fruits.   It is however neceſſary to gather the Peach when thoroughly ripe, but, at
the ſame time not to ſuffer it to hang too long
on the Tree : For as, on the one hand, it
will not acquire its delicious Flavour and
Smell till thoroughly ripe, ſo, on the
other, it will loſe both if ſuffered to hang
on the Tree, after it has attained to a full
Maturity.   Another neceſſary Caution is,
to gather it in fine warm Weather, and near
the Middle of the Day ; becauſe then both
the Flavour and Smell are in the greateſt
Perfection.

It

It is alfo requifite to make Choice of the proper Sorts of Peaches; for there is a remarkable Difference in the Flavour of thefe Fruits. Gardeners reckon above thirty Sorts of Peaches, but not more than half that number are proper for making Ratafia. I fhall therefore give a fhort Defcription of thofe that are moft proper, that the young Diftiller may not be difappointed in making Ratafia from Peaches.

1. The early Purple (called by the *French La Pourprée hâtive*.) This Tree hath fmooth Leaves: The Flowers large, and open: The Fruit is large, round, and of a fine red Colour: The Flefh is white, but very red at the Stone; very full of Juice, which has a rich vinous Flavour. This Peach is ripe about the Middle of *Auguft*.

2. The large, or *French* Mignon. The Leaves of this Tree are fmooth, and the Flowers large and open. The Fruit is a little oblong, generally fwelling out on one Side, and of a fine Colour. The Juice is very fweet, and of a high Flavour; the Flefh white, but very red at the Stone, which is fmall, and eafily feparates from the Flefh. This Peach is ripe in the middle of *Auguft*.

3.

3. The Chevreuse ; or, belle Chevreuse. This Tree hath smooth Leaves; and its Flowers are small and contracted. The Fruit is of a middling Size, a little oblong, and of an elegant Colour. The Flesh is white, but very red at the Stone, from which it separates; full of a rich sugary Juice, and ripens towards the latter End of *August.*

4. The red Magdalen, called by the *French* about *Paris, Magdeleine de Courson.* The Leaves of this Tree are deeply sawed, and the Flowers large and open. The Fruit is large, round, and of a fine red Colour. The Flesh is white, but very red at the Stone, from which it separates. The Juice is very sugary, and of a rich Flavour. It is ripe the latter End of *August.*

5. *Smith's Newington.* This Tree hath sawed Leaves, and large open Flowers. The Fruit is of a middling Size, and of a fine red, next the Sun. The Flesh is very firm and white, but very red at the Stone, to which it closely adhers. It has a rich sugary Juice, and is ripe the latter End of *August.*

6. The Chancellor. The Leaves of this Tree are smooth, and the Flowers small and

and contracted. The Fruit is ſhaped ſome-what like the Belle Chevreuſe, but rounder. The Fleſh is white and melting, and ſe-parates from the Stone, where it is of a fine red Colour. The Skin is very thin, and the Juice remarkably rich. It ripens about the End of *Auguſt*.

7. The Bellegarde; or, as the *French* call it, the *Gallande*. This Tree hath nar-row Leaves, and ſmall contracted Flowers. The Fruit is very large and round, and of a deep purple Colour, on the Side expoſed to the Sun. The Fleſh is white, melting, and ſeparates from the Stone, where it is of a deep red Colour. The Juice is very rich. This Peach is ripe about the begin-ning of *September*.

8. The Bourdine. The Leaves of this Tree are ſmooth, and the Flowers ſmall and contracted. The Fruit is large, round, and of a fine red Colour next the Sun. The Fleſh is white, melting, and ſeparates from the Stone, where it is of a fine red Colour. The Juice is vinous and rich. It is ripe the beginning of *September*, and greatly eſteemed by the curious.

9. The Liſle; or, as the *French* call it, *la petite Violette Hâtive*. This Tree hath ſmooth Leaves, and ſmall contracted Flow-ers.

ers. The Fruit is of a middle Size, and
next the Sun of a fine violet Colour. The
Flesh is of a pale yellow, melting, full of a
rich vinous Juice; but adheres to the Stone,
where it is very red. This Fruit is ripe
the Beginning of *September*.

10. The old *Newington*. The Leaves
of this Tree are sawed, and the Flowers
large and open. The Fruit is fair, large,
and of a beautiful red Colour next the Sun.
The Flesh is white, melting, and closely
adheres to the Stone, where it is of a deep
red Colour. The Juice is very rich and
vinous. It is ripe about the Middle of *September*.

11. The Rambouillet, commonly called
the Rambullion. This Tree has smooth
Leaves, and large open Flowers. The
Fruit is of a middling Size, rather round
than long, deeply divided by a Furrow in
the Middle; of a fine red Colour next the
Sun, but of a light Yellow next the Wall.
The Flesh is melting, of a bright yellow
Colour, except near the Stone, from which
it separates, where it is of a deep red.
The Juice is rich and of a vinous Flavour.
This Fruit ripens about the Middle of *Sep-
tember*.

12.

12. The Pourprée; or, as the *French* generally call it *Pourprée tardive*, the late Purple. The Leaves of this Tree are very large, and fawed, the Shoots ftrong, and the Flowers fmall and contracted. The Flefh, except near the Stone, from which it feparates, and where it is red, is white, melting, and of a rich fugary Juice. It is not ripe till near the End of *September*.

13. The Nevette. The Leaves of this Tree are fawed, and the Flowers fmall and contracted. The Fruit is large, fomewhat longer than round, of a bright red Colour next the Sun, and of a pale yellow on the other. The Flefh is melting, full of a rich Juice, and very red at the Stone, from which it feparates. It ripens about the Middle of *September*, and is efteemed one of the beft Peaches.

14. The Royal. This Tree hath fmooth Leaves, and fmall contracted Flowers. The Fruit is large, round, and of a deep red on the Side expofed to the Sun, but of a pale yellow on the other. The Flefh is white, melting, and full of a rich Juice, of a white Colour, except near the Stone from which it feparates, where it is of a deep red. This Fruit is ripe about the Middle of *September*.

15.

15 The monstrous Pavy of Pompone. The Leaves of this Tree are smooth ; the Flowers large and open. The Fruit is very large and round, many times fourteen Inches in Circumference. The Flesh is white, melting, and closely adheres to the Stone, where it is of a deep red Colour. The Side next the Sun is a beautiful red, and the other of a pale flesh Colour. It ripens about the End of *October*, and when the Autumn is warm, is an excellent Peach.

The above Description of the different Kinds of Peaches proper for making Ratafia, will be of use to the young Artist, as the fine Flavour of this Liquor in a great Measure depends on a proper Choice of the Fruits used in the Composition ; and if the Instructions relating to the Perfections and Ripeness of these Fruits are observed, an excellent Cordial may be easily made in the following manner.

Take your Peaches, bruise them, and instantly strain out their Juice thro' a Piece of strong Linen. In this Juice, without any Mixture of Water, dissolve your Sugar. And when the Sugar is melted, add the Quantity of Spirit. No Spices must be used in this Ratafia, the fine Flavour of the Peach being far preferable to all Spices in the

the World. The Quantity of either the Sugar or Spirit may be augmented or leffened according to your own Judgment, or in Proportion to the Price of your Ratafia.

As foon as the Spirit is added to the dulcified Juice of the Peaches, the whole muft be filtrated thro' a Flannel Bag, put into Bottles clofe ftopped; for the fine Flavour of the Peach will foon be loft unlefs the Bottles are very well corked. Some alfo cover the Cork with Sealing-wax, which is not a bad Caution.

If you would have your Ratafia of a bright red Colour, your muft let your bruifed Peaches ferment a Day or two; by which means the Colour of the Skin, and that of the Flefh near the Stone, will be extracted, and give your Ratafia the Colour defired.

4. *Of Orange-flower Ratafia.*

The Orange-flower has been already defcribed, Page 127. I fhall therefore only add, that the Orange-flowers ufed in making Ratafia fhould be large, in their full Perfection, gathered before the Rifing of the Sun, and carefully picked from their Stalks, &c. Some blanch the Orange-flowers, by putting them into a fmall Quantity of

R   Water,

Water, and boiling them a few Minutes over the Fire. But by this Method the most volatile Parts of the Flower are evaported, by which the Ratafia will lose much of its delicate Flavour.

The best way therefore is to use the Orange-flowers without any previous Boiling.

Recipe for making ten Gallons of Orange-flower Ratafia.

Take of Orange-flowers fresh gathered, and clean picked from their Stalks, &c. five Pounds, and infuse them six Days in five Gallons of clean Proof Spirit. Dissolve fourteen Pounds of Sugar in five Gallons of Water; and after straining the Spirit from the Flowers, mix it with the Syrup, and filtrate the whole thro' a Flannel Bag.

Some instead of common Water use the Orange-flower Water; but it will be necessary in pursuing that Method to take care that the Water be fresh made, and very fragrant; for otherwise instead of improving, you will greatly injure the fine Flavour of your Ratafia.

The foreign Distillers keep two Sorts of Orange-flower Ratafia, one they call *single* and the other *double*. The former is made

according

according to the above Recipe; but in making the latter they ufe double the Quantity of Orange-flowers, and confiderably augment the Proportion of Sugar. It will be needlefs to give a Recipe for making that Sort of Ratafia, which they call *double*, as the Procefs is exactly the fame.

5. *Ratafia of* Portugal *Orange.*

Ratafia may be made from any Sort of Orange; but that of the *Portugal* Orange is reckoned the beft.

The Oranges muft be chofen fair, large, and ripe; and the outer or yellow Peel be carefully taken off. The Juice of the Oranges muft be then preffed out, dulcified with Sugar, and mixed with the Spirit: after which the outer Rinds are to be added, and after a proper Infufion, the whole filtrated through a Flannel Bag.

Recipe for making three Gallons of Portugal *Orange Ratafia.*

Take of the Juice of *Portugal* Oranges two Gallons; clean rectified Spirit one Gallon; four Pounds of Sugar; and the outer Peel of ten Oranges. Let the whole infufe a Fortnight, and then filter the Liquor through a Flannel Bag.

R 2

Some

Some instead of infusing the Peel as directed in the above Recipe, put the Peel into the Spirit, and distil it in Balneum Mariæ; after which they add the Spirit to the dulcified Orange-juice, and filtrate as before.

The foregoing Recipes for making Ratafia from different Fruits, &c. will be sufficient to instruct the young Distiller in the Method necessary to be pursued for making Cordials of this Kind; for it would be tedious to give Formula's for making all the Kinds of Ratafia kept by different Distillers. The Method in all is nearly the same; and the Proportion of Sugar and Spirit may be easily discovered by a few Experiments. I shall therefore conclude this Chapter with giving a Recipe for making what is called by our *English* Distillers Ratafia, tho' a very bad Composition.

Recipe for making ten Gallons of common *Ratafia*.

Take of Nutmegs eight Ounces; bitter Almonds ten Pounds; *Lisbon* Sugar eight Pounds; Ambergrise ten Grains: Infuse these Ingredients three Days in ten Gallons of clean Proof Spirit, and filtre thro' a Flannel Bag for use.

The

The Nutmegs and bitter Almonds must be bruised; and the Ambergrise rubbed with the *Lisbon* Sugar in a Marble Mortar, before they are infused in the Spirit.

CHAP. LIII.

Of Gold Cordial.

THIS Cordial has it Name from Leaf Gold being formerly used in its Compofition; but as later Experiments have abundantly demonftrated that Gold can add nothing to its Virtues, it is now generally omitted.

Recipe for making ten Gallons of Gold Cordial.

Take of the Roots of Angelica, four Pounds; Raifins ftoned, two Pounds; Coriander-feeds, Half a Pound; Caraway-feeds and Cinnamon, of each Half a Pound; Cloves two Ounces; Figs and Liquorice-root, of each one Pound; Proof Spirit eleven Gallons; Water two Gallons: The Angelica, Liquorice, and Figs muft be fliced, before they are added. Digeft two Days, and draw off by gentle Heat, till the Faints begin to rife, hanging in a Piece of Linen faftened to the Mouth of the Worm an

Ounce

Ounce of *English* Saffron. Then diffolve eight Pounds of Sugar in three Quarts of Rofe Water, and add it to the diftilled Liquor. Some Diftillers inftead of Saffron colour their Goods with burnt Sugar, but by this means the Cordial is greatly impaired in its Virtues.

Or,

Take of the Juice of Alchermes five Ounces; Cloves two Ounces and a Half; Mufk and Ambergrife, of each Half a Dram; Loaf Sugar ten Pounds; Proof Spirit eleven Gallons; digeft the whole a Fortnight in a clofe Veffel, and filter thro' a Flannel Bag for ufe. Some add thirty Leaves of Gold; but the Medicine is not at all the better for it.

Either of the above Recipes will produce an excellent Cordial; good in Tremblings, Faintings, and Lownefs of Spirits, &c. Alfo in Naufeas and Griping Pains of the Stomach and Bowels.

CHAP.

C H A P. LIV.

Of Cardamum, or All-fours.

THIS Water has its Name from the four Ingredients in its Compofition; and in fome Countries is greatly ufed by the poorer Sort of People.

Recipe for making ten Gallons of Cardamum.

Take of Pimento, Caraway and Coriander-feeds, and Lemon-peel, of each three Pounds; of Malt Spirits eleven Gallons; Water three Gallons. Draw off with a gentle Fire, dulcify with ordinary Sugar, and make up the Goods, to the Strength you defire with clean Water.

This is rarely called for unlefs by the poor Sort of People, who are induced to ufe it from its Cheapnefs; tho' it is a better Cordial than many drawn from dearer Ingredients. It is an excellent Carminative, and is often fold for Aqua Mirabilis.

CHAP. LV.

Of Geneva.

THERE was formerly kept in the Apothecaries Shops a distilled spirituous Water of Juniper; but the Vulgar being fond of it as a Dram, the Distillers supplanted the Apothecaries, and sold it under the Name of Geneva. The common Sort however is not made from Juniper-berries as it ought to be, but from Oil of Turpentine; the Method of which we shall give in the Sequel of this Chapter.

Juniper-berries are a roundish Fruit, of the Size of a Pea. They wither and wrinkle in the drying, and we meet with them variously corrugated, and usually covered with a bluish resinous Dust when fresh. They should be chosen fresh, plump, full of Pulp, and of a strong Taste and Smell. They are usually imported from *Germany*, tho' we have plenty of the Trees in *England*. It is but small with us, rarely rising to more than three or four Feet in Height, and scarce ever exceeding five or six. Some of the Juniper Shrubs are Males, some Females of the same Species; the Male Shrubs produce in *April* or *May* a small Kind of Juli with Apices on them very large,

large, and full of Farina; the Females produce none of thefe Juli but only the Berries, which do not ripen till the fecond Year, and then do not immediately fall off, fo that it is no uncommon thing to fee three Sets of Berries, or the Berries of three different Years at once on the fame Tree.

If you make ufe of *Englifh* Berries, let them be fully ripe before they are gathered; and in order to preferve them, fpread them very thin on a boarded Floor, leaving the Windows and Doors open, and turn them once a Day till they are dry; after which pack them up in Barrels, fo that no Air may come to them, and they will keep good all the Year. Some, when they are dry, throw them altogether in a Heap in a Corner of the Room, where they continue till wanted for ufe; but the Berries will not keep fo well by this Method as by being packed in Cafks; they are fubject to contract a Mouldinefs, which will give a Tafte to the Goods, greatly to their Difadvantage.

Some Diftillers as foon as their Berries are gathered, put them into Cafks, and cover them with Spirits of Wine; by this Method the Berries are indeed well preferved, without any Danger of contracting an ill Smell, which they are very apt to

do

do by the other Methods unlefs the greateft Care be taken ; but then it muft be remembered, that the Spirit will extract great Part of their effential Oil, in which their Virtues: confift, and confequently the Berries themfelves will be rendered of little Value. If, therefore, you preferve your Berries in this manner, you fhould put into each Cafk or Jarr, only the Quantity you ufe for one Charge of your Still ; and when you have occafion to ufe them, put both the Spirits and Berries into your Alembic.

Thus your Berries will be finely preferved, without any Lofs either of their effential Oil, or the Spirits made ufe of to preferve.

Recipe for making ten Gallons of Geneva.

Take of Juniper-berries three Pounds, Proof Spirit ten Gallons; Water four Gallons. Draw off by a gentle Fire till the Faints begin to rife, and make up your Goods to the Strength required with clean Water.

The Diftillers generally call thofe Goods which are made up Proof by the Name of Royal Geneva; for the common Sort is much below Proof, ten Gallons of Spirit
being

being fufficient for fifteen Gallons of Geneva. Nay, what is generally fold at the common Alehoufes is made in the following manner.

Take of the ordinary Malt Spirits ten Gallons; Oil of Turpentine two Ounces, Bay Salt three Handfuls. Draw off by a gentle Fire till the Faints begin to rife, and make up your Goods to the Strength required with clean Water.

In this manner is the common Geneva made, and it is fuprizing that People fhould accuftom themfelves to drink it for pleafure.

There is a Sort of this Liquor called *Holland*'s Geneva, from it being imported from *Holland*, which is greatly efteemed.

The Ingredients ufed by the *Dutch* are, however, the fame as thofe given in the firft Recipe of this Chapter, only inftead of Malt Spirit they ufe *French* Brandy. In the firft Part of this Treatife we have fufficiently fhewn the Nature of *French* Brandy, and in what its Excellence confifts; and, alfo, that by the Help of a clean Spirit, Cordial Waters may be made with the fame Goodnefs as thofe drawn with *French* Brandy.

a miftake, Hollands Gin is rectifydfrom Malt fpirits —

Brandy. If therefore the Diftiller be careful in diftilling and rectifying his Malt Spirit, he may make Geneva equal to that of the *Dutch*, provided it be kept to a proper Age; for all fpirituous Liquors contract a Softnefs and Mellownefs by Age, impoffible to be imitated by Art.

CHAP. LVI.

Of Cherry Brandy.

THIS Liquor is greatly called for in the Country; and is made different ways. Some prefs out the Juice of the Cherries, and having dulcified it with Sugar, add as much Spirit to it as the Goods will bear, or the Price it is intended to be fold for. But the common Method is to put the Cherries clean picked into a Cafk, with a proper Quantity of Proof Spirit, and after ftanding eighteen or twenty Days, the Goods are drawn off into another Cafk for Sale, and about two thirds of the firft Quantity of Spirits poured into the Cafk upon the Cherries, This is fuffered to ftand about a Month to extract the whole Virtue from the Cherries, after which it is drawn off as before; and the Cherries preffed to take out the Spirit they had abforbed. The Proportion of Cherries and Spirit is not very nicely obferved; the general Rule
is

is to let the Caſk be about half filled with
Cherries, and then filled up with Proof
Spirits.　Some add to every twenty Gallons
of Spirit half an Ounce of Cinnamon, an
Ounce of Cloves, and about three Pounds
of Sugar, by which the Flavour of the
Goods is conſiderably increaſed.　But in
order to ſave Expences, not only the Spices
and Sugar are generally omitted, but alſo
great Part of the Cherries, and the Defi-
cience ſupplied by the Juice of Elder-ber-
ries.　Your own Reaſon therefore, and the
Price you can ſell your Goods for, muſt
direct you in the Choice of your Ingredients.

By the ſame Method you may make Rafberry Brandy; and if the Colour of the
Goods be not deep enough, it may be improved by an Addition of Cherry Brandy.

CHAP. LVII.

Of Honey Water.

THIS Water has its Name from the
Honey in its Compoſition; tho' that
Ingredient is but of very little Service to the
Water, if made according to the uſual Me-
thod.

Recipe

Recipe for making a Gallon of Honey Water.

Take of the beſt Honey and Coriander-ſeeds, of each one Pound; Cloves, one Ounce and a Half; Nutmegs and Gum Benjamin, of each an Ounce; Vanilloes Number four. The yellow Rind of three large Lemons: Bruiſe the Cloves, Nutmegs, Coriander-ſeed, and Benjamin; cut the Vanilloes in pieces, and put all into a Glaſs Alembic, with one Gallon of clean rectified Spirit, and after digeſting forty eight Hours, draw off the Spirit in Balneum Mariæ. To a Gallon of the above Spirit, add of damaſk Roſe Water and Orange-flower Water, of each a Pound and a Half; Muſk and Ambergriſe of each five Grains. Grind the Muſk and Ambergriſe with ſome of the Water in a Glaſs Mortar, and afterwards put all together into a digeſting Veſſel, ſhaking them well together, and let them circulate three Days and three Nights in a gentle Heat: Then let all cool; filter and keep the Water in Bottles well ſtopped for uſe.

This Water was firſt made by that faithful Chemiſt Mr. *George Wilſon*, for King *James* II. It is an Antiparalitic, ſmooths the Skin, and gives one of the moſt agreeable Scents imaginable. Forty or ſixty
Drops

Drops put into a Pint of clean Water, are fufficient for wafhing the Hands and Face; and the fame Proportion to Punch, or any Cordial Water, gives a very agreeable Flavour.

CHAP. LVIII.

Of Unequalled Water, generally fold by the French Name l'Eau fans Pareille.

There are two Sorts of this Water, one drawn confiderably below Proof, and rendered fine by Filtration, and the other without the Faints, the Receiver being removed as foon as they begin to rife. The latter is much the beft, tho' dearer than the former.

Recipe for making a Gallon of the common Eau fans Pareille.

Take the outer Peels of twelve Citrons, three Quarts of fine Proof Spirit, and a Quart of Water. Put all into a Glafs Alembic, and diftil to a Drynefs in Balneum Mariæ; filtre the Water, and put it into Bottles well ftopped.

This is the common Sort, and what is generally fold here under the Name *Eau fans Pareille.*

Recipe

Recipe for making a Gallon of the best Sort of Eau sans Pareille.

Take of the Essence of Cedrat, Bergamot, Orange, and Lemon, of each two Drams; rectified Spirit a Gallon; Water two Quarts. Put all into a Glass Alembic, and distil in Balneum Mariæ till the Faints begin to rise, when the Receiver must be immediately removed.

Some to save the Trouble and Expence of Distillation, mix the Essences with the Spirit of Wine, in the manner before mentioned in the Chapter for making Hungary Water; but this is greatly inferior to that made by Distillation.

CHAP. LIX.

Of the *Water of Bouquet.*

THIS Water has its Name from its Inventor, and is greatly esteemed abroad for its Smell. It is indeed drawn from the most odoriferous Flowers, and therefore it is no wonder that it is held in great Esteem.

Recipe

Recipe for making a Gallon of Bouquet's Water.

Take of the Flowers of white Lillies, and *Spanish* Jeffamin, of each Half a Pound; Orange-flowers and thofe of the Jonquil and Pink of each four Ounces; damafk Rofes one Pound. Let thofe be frefh gathered, and immediately put into a Glafs Alembic with a Gallon of clean Proof Spirit, and two Quarts of Water. Place the Alembic in Balneum Mariæ, draw off till the Faints begin to rife. You may ufe Spirit of Wine, inftead of Proof Spirit; but it will be abfolutely neceffary that it be entirely inodorous; for otherwife your Water will fall fhort of the defired Perfection.

CHAP. LX.

Of Cyprus Water.

THIS Water is only a dilute Tincture of Ambergrife; but as it is ufed by thofe who are fond of that Perfume, and known by the Name of Cyprus Water, or *Eau de Chypre*, I would not omit giving the Recipe here, intending to give a full Account of Ambergrife in a fucceeding Chapter.

S

Recipe

Recipe for making a Gallon of Cyprus Water.

Take of the Essence of Ambergrise Half an Ounce; put it into a Glass Alembic with a Gallon of Spirit of Wine and two Quarts of Water. Place the Alembic in Balneum Mariæ, and draw off till the Faints begin to rise.

CHAP. LXI.

Of Vestal Water, or Eau de Vestale.

THIS is a very agreeable Water, and has been long in use in several Parts of *Europe.*

Recipe for a Gallon of Vestal Water.

Take of the Seeds of Daucus Creticus or Candy Carrots, two Ounces; Spirit of Wine a Gallon; Water two Quarts. Distil in Balneum Mariæ till the Faints begin to rise. Then add to the Spirit drawn over an Ounce of the Essence of Lemons, and four Drops of the Essence of Ambergrise; redistil in Balneum Mariæ, and keep the Water in Bottles well stoped for use.

CHAP.

CHAP. LXII.

Of Beauty Water, or Eau de Beauté.

THIS Water has it Name from its ufe in wafhing the Face, and giving an agreeable Smell. It is drawn from Thyme and Marjoram, which gives it a very elegant Odour.

Recipe for making a Gallon of Beauty Water.

Take of the flowery Tops of Thyme and Marjoram, of each one Pound ; Proof Spirits five Quarts; Water one Quart. Draw off in Balneum Mariæ, till the Faints begin to rife, and keep it clofe ftopped for ufe.

CHAP. LXIII.

Of Royal Water.

THIS Water has its Name from being confidered as the moft excellent of all fcented Waters. It is compounded of the Cedrat, Nutmegs and Mace, from whence the moft elegant Smell is produced; and no Water is at prefent thought equal to this. There are two Sorts of Royal Water, one produced by a fingle Diftillation, and the other by a double Diftillation,

and

and thence called rectified, or double diftilled Royal Water.

Recipe for a Gallon of Royal Water.

Take of Mace one Ounce; Nutmegs
Half an Ounce; Essence of Cedrat, or Ber-
gamot two Drams: Put these into a Glass
Alembic (after bruising the Spices) with five
Quarts of fine Proof Spirit, and draw off
one Gallon in Balneum Mariæ.

Recipe for making a Gallon of double distilled Royal Water.

Take of Mace one Ounce; Nutmegs
Half an Ounce; bruise them, and put them
into an Alembic with six Quarts of fine
Proof Spirit, and draw off five Quarts
with a gentle Fire. Then take the Spirit
drawn off and put it into a Glass Alembic,
with two Drams of the Essence of Cedrat,
or Bergamot, and draw off a Gallon in
Balneum Mariæ.

Either of these Recipes will produce an
elegant Water; but the latter greatly exceeds the former.

CHAP.

CHAP. LXIV.

Of the Tincture, or Effence of Ambergrife, Mufk and Civet.

1. AUTHORS have been long divided with regard to the Origin of Ambergrife; fome taking it for a vegetable Juice, which either dropped into the Water from the Trunks or Branches of fome Trees growing on the Sea-coaft, or exudated from their Roots which ran out of the Earth into the Sea; fome for an animal Production, and formed either by a fecret Procefs from Honey-combs, or the Dung of Birds; and others have very circumftantially recorded that it is produced in the Whale. Thefe Opinions are however now looked upon as falfe; Ambergrife being univerfally allowed to be a Mineral Production, of the Number of Bitumens. It is a light and frothy Subftance, which generally bubbles up out of the Earth in a fluid Form, principally under Water, where it is by Degrees hardened into the Maffes we fee it in.

Ambergrife in its natural, or common Form is a lax and coarfe Subftance of an irregular Structure, friable, and fo light as to fwim upon Water. It is of a pale gray Colour, with a faint Tinge of brown in it; but Pieces perfectly and uniformly of this

Colour

Colour are rare, what we usually meet with is composed of whitish, yellowish, and blackish Granules; and in Proportion as there is more or less of this whitish Matter in these Masses, it is more or less scented and valuable. It is found in Pieces of perfectly irregular Figures, and from the Bigness of a Pea to those of ten, twenty, or more Pounds; nay there have been Masses found of more than two Hundred Weight.

It should be chosen in clean and not over friable Pieces, of a pale grey Colour, and as uniform as possible in its Structure, with small black Specks within.

There are two Sorts of Essences made from this Perfume; one without Addition of any other odoriferous Substance, and the other from Ambergrise compounded with Musk and Civit.

Recipe for making the Essence of Ambergrise.

Take of Ambergrise and white Sugar-candy, of each three Drams; grind them well together in a Glass Mortar, adding to them by slow Degrees, five Ounces of rectified Spirit of Wine, digest the whole in a Martrass (represented Fig. 8.) well stopped for four Days, and then separate the clear Tincture or Essence, which keep in a Bottle well stopt for use.   *Re-*

Recipe for making the compound Eſſence of Ambergriſe.

Take of Ambergriſe and white Sugar-candy of each two Drams; Muſk twelve Grains; Civet two Grains; grind all theſe well together in a Glaſs Mortar, adding by Degrees four Ounces of rectified Spirit of Wine; digeſt and ſeparate the clear Eſſence for uſe, as in the preceding Recipe.

2. Muſk is a dry, light, and friable Subſtance; of a dark blackiſh Colour, with ſome Tinge of a purpliſh or blood Colour in it. It is ſoft, and ſomewhat ſmooth and unctuous to the Touch, and of a highly perfumed Smell. It is brought to us ſewed up in a Kind of Bladders or Caſes of Skin, covered with a browniſh Hair, which are the real Bags in which the Muſk is lodged while on the Animal. Muſk ſhould be choſen of a very ſtrong Scent, and in dry found Bladders; and muſt be kept cloſe ſhut down in a Leaden Box, by which means it will retain its Smell, and not grow too dry.

Recipe for making the Eſſence of Musk.

Take of Muſk and white Sugar-candy of each one Dram; rub them well together in a Marble Mortar, adding by Degrees during the rubbing five Ounces of rectified Spirit of Wine: Put the whole into a Matrass, digest three Days in a gentle Heat, and pour off the clear Essence, which keep in a Bottle well stopt for use. Some add a few Grains of Civet to their Essence of Musk, which considerably augments the Fineness of the Perfume.

3. Civet is produced, like Musk, in Bags growing to the lower Part of the Belly of an Animal. It is of different Colours from a pure lively whitish, to a black; but the nearer it approaches to the white the better it is; of an extremely strong Smell, and a bitterish pungent Taste.

The Essence of Civet is rarely used alone, but of great service in making Additions to other odoriferous Waters, and therefore I shall here give the Method of making it.

Recipe for making the Essence of Civet.

Take of Civet and double refined Sugar, of each two Drams; rub them well together in a Glass Mortar, adding by Degrees five Ounces of rectified Spirit of Wine: Put the whole into a Matrass, digest three Days in a gentle Heat, and pour off the clear Essence for use. Tho' the Essences

in

in this Chapter are, properly fpeaking, Chemical Preparations, and therefore foreign to the Bufinefs of the Diftiller; yet as they are often added to perfumed Waters, and eafily made, I thought the above Recipes would not be unacceptable to the Reader.

CHAP. LXV.

Of Faints, and the Ufes they may be applied to.

IN many of the preceding Recipes I have ordered the Receiver to be removed as foon as the Faints begin to rife; becaufe otherwife the Goods would contract a difagreeable Tafte and Smell. It is not however to be underftood that thefe Faints are to be thrown away, nor the Working of the Still immediately ftopped; for they are far from being of no Value, notwithftanding they would be of great Difadvantage if fuffered to run among the more fpirituous Parts of the Goods before drawn off. As foon therefore as you find the clear Colour of the Goods begins to change of a bluifh or whitifh Colour, remove the Receiver, place another under the Nofe of the Worm, and continue the Diftillation as long as the Liquor running from the Worm is fpirituous, which may be known by pouring a little of

it

it on the Still Head, and applying a lighted Candle to it ; for if it is spirituous it will burn, but otherwise not. When the Faints will no longer burn on the Still Head, put out the Fire, and pour the Faints in a Cask for that Purpose ; and when, from repeated Distillations, you have procured a sufficient Quantity of these Faints, let the Still be charged with them almost to the Top. Then throw into the Still three or four Pounds of Salt, and draw off as you would any other Charge as long as the Spirit extracted is of a sufficient Strength ; after which the Receiver is to be removed, and the Faints saved by themselves as before.

The Spirits thus extracted from the Faints will serve in several Compositions as well as fresh ; but they are generally used in Aniseed Water, because the predominant Taste of the Aniseeds will entirely cover that they had before acquired from other Ingredients.

THE

THE
INDEX

A.

Anil-

The INDEX.

Cardamum

Definition

The INDEX.

Distillation

The INDEX.

T   Orange,

The INDEX.

The INDEX.

T 2   *Simple*

The INDX.

T.

The INDEX.

Water

The INDEX.

The INDEX.

F I N I S.

CPSIA information can be obtained at www.ICGtesting.com
Printed in the USA
BVOW02s2029180614

356716BV00005B/299/P